EDNA O'BRIEN

EDNA O'BRIEN

W

EDNA
O'BRIEN

Amanda Greenwood

Northcote House
in association with the
British Council

© Copyright 2003 by Amanda Greenwood

First published in 2003 by Northcote House Publishers Ltd, Horndon, Tavistock, Devon, PL19 9NQ, United Kingdom.
Tel: +44 (01822) 810066. Fax: +44 (01822) 810034.

British Library Cataloguing-in-Publication Data
A catalogue record for this book is available from the British Library

ISBN 0-7463-1022-6 hardcover
ISBN 0-7463-0967-8 paperback

Typeset by TW Typesetting, Plymouth, Devon
Printed and bound in the United Kingdom by
Athenaeum Press Ltd., Gateshead Tyne & Wear

This book is dedicated with love to the memory of my father, Gordon Simpson 1933–1999

and to Kevin Fitzsimons, with love and thanks

Contents

Acknowledgements

I am indebted to Isobel Armstrong, Clare Hanson, Sophia Hillan, Marion Shaw, Gerry Smyth and Jane Thomas for all their encouragement and advice.

Biographical Outline

1930	Born 15 December in Tuamgraney, County Clare, Ireland to Michael (a farmer) and Lena.
1936	Attends the National School in Scarriff, County Clare.
1941	Attends the Convent of Mercy at Loughrea, County Galway.
1946	Attends the Pharmaceutical College of Ireland, Dublin; qualifies as a Licentiate.
1948	Begins writing for the *Irish Press*.
1951	Marries writer Ernest Gebler (divorced 1964).
1952	Birth of son, Carlo.
1954	Birth of son, Sasha.
1959	Relocates to London. Writes *The Country Girls* in three weeks.
1960	Publication of *The Country Girls*, which wins the Kingsley Amis Award.
1962	Publication of *The Lonely Girl*. First performance of *A Cheap Bunch of Nice Flowers* at New Arts Theatre, London, on 20 November.
1963	Publication of *A Cheap Bunch of Nice Flowers* in *Plays of the Year..*
1964	Publication of *Girls in their Married Bliss*. First screenplay of *Girl with Green Eyes*, adapted from *The Lonely Girl*.
1965	Publication of *August is a Wicked Month*.
1966	Publication of *Casualties of Peace*. Writes screenplay *Time Lost and Time Remembered*, based on short story 'A Woman at the Seaside', in collaboration with Desmond Davis.

1968   Publication of short story collection *The Love Object*. Writes screenplay *Three Into Two Won't Go*, adapted from the novel by Andrea Newman.
1970   Publication of *A Pagan Place*, which wins *Yorkshire Post* Award for Novel of the Year.
1971   Publication of screenplay *Zee & Co.*
1972   Production of *Zee & Co.* as *X, Y, and Z*. Stage adaptation of *A Pagan Place*, 2 November at Royal Court Theatre, London. Publication of *Night*.
1974   Publication of *A Scandalous Woman and Other Stories*.
1976   Publication of *Johnny I Hardly Knew You*.
1977   Publication of *Arabian Days*.
1978   Publication of *Mrs Reinhardt and Other Stories*.
1979   Publication of *Some Irish Loving*.
1980   Performance of *Virginia* at Stratford, Ontario.
1981   Publication of *The Dazzle*, *Virginia* and *James and Nora: A Portrait of Joyce's Marriage*.
1982   Publication of *Returning: A Collection of Tales*.
1984   Publication of *A Fanatic Heart: Selected Stories*.
1986   Publication of *The Country Girls: Trilogy and Epilogue* and *Tales for the Telling: Irish Folk and Fairy Stories*.
1988   Publication of *The High Road*.
1989   Publication of poetry collection, *On the Bone*.
1990   Publication of short story collection *Lantern Slides*, which wins the *Los Angeles Times* Book Award.
1992   Publication of *Time and Tide*, which wins *Los Angeles Times* Book Award.
1994   Publication of *House of Splendid Isolation*.
1996   Publication of *Down by the River*.
1999   6 July awarded Honorary Doctorate of Literature by the Faculty of the Humanities, Queen's University, Belfast. Publication of *James Joyce* and *Wild Decembers*. Opening of the play *Our Father* at the Almeida Theatre, London.
2002   Publication of *In the Forest*.

Preface

Edna O'Brien is a prolific and deeply engaging writer whose novels and short stories have received many literary awards to date, yet though she has been the subject of a wealth of articles and essays no monograph has been published on her work since Grace Eckley's *Edna O'Brien* in 1974. In writing this study I have focused on aspects of O'Brien's work such as her ongoing deconstructions of 'femininity', 'maternity' and 'masculinity' – particularly with reference to Ireland – and on her increasing concern for the 'maternal body' of the land. I have questioned recurrent perceptions of O'Brien as a lightweight chronicler of women's sexual and emotional experience, highlighting the extent to which this is culturally and historically located throughout her work.

Inevitably there are significant and regrettable omissions. I have concentrated on the novels at the expense of the short stories, which have been well documented elsewhere. O'Brien's analysis of the mother–son relationship throughout these novels deserves a monograph in itself. The edited collection *Some Irish Loving* (1979) offers invaluable insights into literary influences on O'Brien whilst demonstrating her own extensive knowledge of canonical and other Irish literatures, and her poetry merits further investigation. But despite the limitations of this study it has been my very great privilege to write it.

Abbreviations and References

AWM	*August is a Wicked Month* (London: Jonathan Cape, 1965)
CG	*The Country Girls* (Harmondsworth: Penguin, 1963)
CJIS, 22:2	*Canadian Journal of Irish Studies: Special Edition on Edna O'Brien*, vol. 22, no. 2 (December 1996)
CP	*Casualties of Peace* (Harmondsworth: Penguin, 1968)
DR	*Down by the River* (London: Weidenfeld & Nicolson, 1996)
FH	*A Fanatic Heart* (London: Weidenfeld & Nicolson, 1984)
GGE	*Girl with Green Eyes* (Harmondsworth: Penguin, 1964)
GMB	*Girls in their Married Bliss* (Harmondsworth: Penguin, 1967)
HR	*The High Road* (Harmondsworth: Penguin, 1989)
HSI	*House of Splendid Isolation* (London: Weidenfeld & Nicolson, 1994)
IF	*In the Forest* (London: Weidenfeld & Nicolson, 2002)
JJ	*James Joyce* (London: Weidenfeld & Nicolson, 1999)
MI	*Mother Ireland* (London: Weidenfeld & Nicolson, 1976)
N	*Night* (Harmondsworth: Penguin, 1992)
PP	*A Pagan Place* (London: Weidenfeld & Nicolson, 1972)
V	*Virginia* (London: Hogarth Press, 1981)
WD	*Wild Decembers* (London: Weidenfeld & Nicolson, 1999)

1

Edna O'Brien and Her Critics

In 1997 the National Portrait Gallery exhibited Bill Brandt's study of Edna O'Brien alongside portraits of Doris Lessing and Germaine Greer, implicitly acknowledging her status as a contemporary woman writer of literary and cultural significance. The Gallery's caption read: 'Since her first novel *The Country Girls* (1960), O'Brien has addressed the subject of women in society, of solitude and sexual repression'.

I have taken the Gallery's positioning of Edna O'Brien as a starting point for this study because it highlights a perceived gap between 'society' and 'solitude' which for the last three decades has characterized responses by the media and the literary establishment to this particular writer and her work. O'Brien has been read as a writer whose work disregards 'social institutions and ties', 'living tradition [and] ideas', concentrating solely upon the sexual awakenings and disappointments of her protagonists. In 1972 the same reviewer who lamented O'Brien's apparent failure to 'move outside the magic circle of women's emotional problems' also revealed that: 'Reading Edna O'Brien's fiction, I've been surprised by perceptions of what I thought no one else knew – and I wasn't telling'.[1] Almost thirty years on O'Brien continues – despite her wide-ranging and ongoing experiments with form, genre and content – to be constructed largely as a repetitive chronicler of romantic love. A reviewer of her 1999 biography of James Joyce remarked, for example, that 'all Edna O'Brien's effort proves is that lightweight novelists should stick to what they do best'.[2]

In order to understand the ambivalent attitude of the literary establishment towards O'Brien, it is necessary to address the

1

problematic issues of her public persona and – related to this – her position as a diasporic Irish woman writer. The question of O'Brien's Irishness will be specifically addressed in chapter 2. As Rebecca Pelan astutely points out, O'Brien's persona has contributed towards 'the relegation of [her] writing to the realm of popular fiction, a ... category which allows the content of her writing to go virtually unnoticed'.[3] It is difficult to gauge the extent to which O'Brien undermines her own position as a 'serious' writer, and how much it is undermined for her. She has advertised shampoo and appeared on television chat shows, and has been associated since the 1960s with media personalities such as Rita Tushingham, who played Caithleen in *Girl with Green Eyes*, the film adaptation of O'Brien's second novel *The Lonely Girl*. When she was asked to unveil a commemorative plaque to James Joyce at a house in Kensington where he briefly lived, she reflected that 'she'd better get her hair done or something for the occasion'.[4] O'Brien herself is all too aware of 'image' as a double-edged sword, remarking that 'if you happen to have your hair done, well, then you can't be a "serious" writer'.[5]

O'Brien's capacity for self-irony has been recurrently ignored in the face of her perceived humourlessness. In a review of *House of Splendid Isolation* – a novel which was never going to offer much in the way of light relief, given that it addresses terrorism, abortion and political martyrdom – Joan Smith made the disparaging comment that 'too much posing as a tragedy queen has turned [O'Brien] deaf to her own bathetic efforts'.[6] It seems that O'Brien cannot win. Writing about 'women's emotional problems' she is dismissed as narrow in scope; addressing political issues she is branded a poseuse. In 1995 O'Brien wrote an objective and articulate open letter to Tony Blair, questioning his perceived 'reticen[ce] about Ireland' and arguing that '[Gerry] Adams has a relevant place in the political caucus'.[7] O'Brien's public support of Adams was greeted, however, with responses such as 'Edna O'Brien knows a strong, flawed and emotionally unavailable hero when she sees one' and 'Edna O'Brien [is] the Barbara Cartland of long-distance Republicanism'.[8]

Why has O'Brien's access to political and literary arenas been denied? Her agent, David Godwin, echoes Rebecca

Pelan's identification of the 'persona' as problematic. Comparing O'Brien to Lessing,[9] he argues that 'because Edna is a more glamorous woman sometimes people don't take her so seriously'.[10] Even allowing for some degree of partiality, Godwin has a point. Nicholas Wroe's article – which cited his comments – also included, with no apparent sense of irony, observations on O'Brien's 'brown velvet Jasper Conran dress' and 'still seductively soft Irish voice'. Wroe also speculates on O'Brien's private life, offering a titillating commentary on her life in the 1960s: 'It seemed she knew everyone, drank champagne with most of them and, if even half the rumours are to be believed, slept with quite a few'. Wroe's article perpetuates these very 'rumours'.

Edna O'Brien is aware of her own dilemma; one reviewer records her as having said 'I'm a serious writer. Take more notice of the books than how I look'.[11] Yet the same review begins: 'Her red hair is tousled immaculately, her pale, powdered skin is flawless. She puts her small-boned hands in her lap, opens wide her clear, green eyes and awaits the first question . . . Here she is, a veritable flame-haired temptress'. The language of this review constructs O'Brien as self-consciously manipulative, implying not only that she is obsessed with her appearance, but that she is calculating and underhand. 'Tousled immaculately' does suggest duplicity. O'Brien's claim to be a 'serious writer' is undermined without acknowledgement.

Throughout my analysis of O'Brien's persona I am going to concentrate on reviews of *House of Splendid Isolation*, since these highlight issues surrounding O'Brien's position as a diasporic Irish Catholic woman writer which will be addressed more specifically in chapter 2. *House of Splendid Isolation* was published in 1994, and is the first of a trilogy on contemporary Ireland which also comprises *Down by the River* (1996) and *Wild Decembers* (1999). *House of Splendid Isolation* tells the story of Josie, an elderly widow living in a crumbling 'big house' who forms a relationship with a republican terrorist, McGreevy, when he invades her property whilst on the run from the Garda. The novel was carefully researched; O'Brien visited and consulted with the late Dominic McGlinchey, who was in prison following charges of terrorism. Despite this, reviews

3

and even so-called literary criticism persisted in focusing on O'Brien as an ageing *femme fatale*, assuming that her interest in republicanism arose not so much from concern with Irish politics and history, but rather from an attraction to the 'flawed' and 'emotionally unavailable' hero supposedly typified by Gerry Adams.

The mixed reviews of *House of Splendid Isolation* say at least as much about what the media and critical establishment want and need O'Brien to be as they do about her book. One interview was titled 'Looking for Trouble',[12] ostensibly referring to the novel's focus on 'the troubles' in Northern Ireland whilst simultaneously suggesting that O'Brien was 'asking for it' in tackling such heavyweight subject matter.[13] The interview's subtitle, 'Edna O'Brien on terrorism, old age and lust', planted the notion that this was 'really' a book about 'the end of sexuality and desirability'.[14] The interviewer did ask O'Brien directly whether she was 'describing some of her own fears'. Joan Smith simultaneously denigrated O'Brien's previous output, referring to 'wearyingly familiar territory', and dismissed her departure from the domestic sphere by arguing that 'what O'Brien has attempted in this novel . . . is to graft a narrative about terrorism onto one of her familiar laments for lost youth and frustrated passion'. Another reviewer assumed that O'Brien was addressing political issues in a cynical attempt 'to shore up a sagging reputation', pointing out that she is known largely for her 'fey, charming and obviously autobiographical earlier works'.[15]

'Obviously autobiographical' needs to be addressed, since this is a view of O'Brien's output which recurs in literary criticism as well as in interviews and reviews. The reductive tendency to identify the author with her female protagonists has been largely instrumental in her relegation to 'popular fiction'. Those who wish to read her work as dressed-up autobiography have not been discouraged by her ongoing experiments with form and genre. The accessible first-person narrative of *The Country Girls* (1960), the deployment of *écriture feminine* in *Night* (1972) and the political focus of *House of Splendid Isolation* have all been read as autobiographical outpourings. Even the play *Virginia* has been received simply as projection, with one critic commenting that 'the woman on

4

stage was Edna O'Brien, not Virginia Woolf'.[16] ('The woman on stage' was actually Maggie Smith.) As Maureen Grogan succinctly remarks, 'there seems to be little consideration of the possibility that the emotional content of [O'Brien's] work is a deliberate artistic choice, not simply an uncontrolled eruption of the writer's experience'.[17]

The identification of Edna O'Brien with her female protagonists is a response common not only to journalists and reviewers but also to literary critics. As early as 1974 Grace Eckley noted that:

> Miss O'Brien's novels – written for the most part in the first person – give the impression that they are a personal odyssey beginning with the background in County Clare, the convent school education, removal to London, birth of children, and dissolution of marriage. Several critics accurately sensed a deep personal wound that provokes revenge against men through the diabolical male characters ... and should have recognized Ernest Gebler's [O'Brien's former husband's] initials in the name Eugene Gaillard.[18]

Although Eckley's study was produced within the context of 1970s Anglo-American feminism, with its focus on empiricism, she does recognize the limitations inherent in reading O'Brien's texts as 'personal odyssey'. Eckley's acknowledgement of the problematics of biographical reading is somewhat literal – she points out, for example, that 'although in several of her novels and short stories, the heroine's mother is dead, Miss O'Brien's mother is still living', and that 'she seldom makes a writer one of her characters'.[19] Yet despite the naivety of Eckley's argument her caveat against the biographical reading transcends the limitations of many of O'Brien's more recent critics. In 1987, for example, Peggy O'Brien published an article entitled 'The Silly and the Serious: An Assessment of Edna O'Brien'. It is significant that the title's reference is to the writer rather than to her works; Peggy O'Brien addresses the issue of 'persona' only obliquely, but her construction of polarities reveals much about her expectations as a reader. Peggy O'Brien focuses principally on *The Country Girls* trilogy; her expressed intention is 'to understand rather than judge an author's

5

psychology that avoids certain opportunities and embraces others'.[20] This results in a reading which identifies the author not so much with as through character, so that textual analysis is deployed towards low-level psychoanalysis of O'Brien herself. Using the disclaimer that 'one could be forgiven for seeing O'Brien's works as autobiographical' Peggy O'Brien proceeds to have her critical cake and eat it, praising 'the artist's special skill in portraying adolescence' whilst suggesting that 'the authorial identity is arrested in its development and has difficulty in imagining mature adults with clarity'. Arguing that O'Brien's narrative technique lacks control, Peggy O'Brien maintains that:

> If one reads O'Brien for the extreme effect those first intimates, mother and father, have on her authorial psyche, then various aspects of her fictional practice become comprehensible ... The collusion between author and character is essentially a blurring of the boundaries between individual and parental identities; and the unresolved nature of these primary relationships accounts for O'Brien's overall obsessiveness.[21]

'Obsessiveness' refers here to O'Brien's recurrent concentration on 'primary relationships', which Peggy O'Brien identifies as the author's 'effort to redeem herself, to become whole'. While making heavy weather of a literary output which has been popularized largely because of its accessibility, this fails to offer any serious analysis of the gap between 'the silly' and 'the serious'.

In 1982 Darcy O'Brien's essay 'Edna O'Brien: a kind of Irish childhood' contributed further to autobiographical readings of O'Brien's texts. Like Peggy O'Brien, Darcy O'Brien acknowledges that 'it is easy enough to trace the realities of this childhood through Miss O'Brien's fiction'. He proceeds to do exactly this, justifying his somewhat crude analysis of O'Brien's output by transferring responsibility to the reader:

> One's guess is that many if not most of Edna O'Brien's readers must have contemplated the relation between these heroines and their creator. Never mind whether such contemplation be indecent, speculative, out of proper bounds, or unworthy of the professional critic; it is a question that arises and begs to be addressed.[22]

This critic's contradictory attempts at critical detachment – 'one's guess' – do little to disguise his own inability to read

O'Brien's works as other than autobiography. Despite his acknowledgement of the impropriety of autobiographical readings, he goes on to speculate about 'the initials of the brutal husband in *Girls in their Married Bliss*'. Echoing Eckley, he ingeniously works out that these 'correspond to those of [O'Brien's] former husband'. Darcy O'Brien does see O'Brien's 'autobiographical fiction' as culturally significant, pointing out that because O'Brien's predecessors in Irish women's writing were Anglo-Irish – Maria Edgeworth, Lady Gregory and Elizabeth Bowen, for example – she was 'the first country girl to write of [her] experience'. This observation could have offered a starting point for a sustained analysis of O'Brien's position within the literary canon; Darcy O'Brien's essay appeared alongside contributions on Lessing, Murdoch and Drabble. However, the implications of the inclusion of Darcy O'Brien's essay – specifically the identification of O'Brien as a 'serious' writer – are severely undermined by the unrelenting conflation of author and character revealed by the designation of O'Brien herself as 'country girl'.

O'Brien's own view on autobiographical readings is that 'Whether a novel is autobiographical or not does not matter. What is important is the truth in it and the way that truth is expressed'.[23] In this respect O'Brien's early novels anticipate postmodernist writers such as Jeanette Winterson, whose comment on the issue of whether *Oranges Are Not the Only Fruit* is or is not autobiographical is: 'No not at all and yes of course'.[24] Toril Moi has argued that, when looking at the 'literary' and 'autobiographical' texts of a single author, 'the point is not to treat one text as the implicit meaning of another, but rather to read them all with and against each other in order to bring out their points of tension, contradictions and similarities'.[25] Moi's proposed methodology offers new possibilities for reading a writer as versatile as O'Brien, and for ensuring that texts as diverse as *The Country Girls* trilogy, the experimental *A Pagan Place* and *Night*, the play *Virginia* and the semi-autobiographical *Mother Ireland* are not collectively reduced to 'autobiography'.

So how might O'Brien's texts be more productively read? The 1990s saw some significant departures in O'Brien criticism derived from post-colonial, psychoanalytic and

7

feminist theories. Mary Salmon's analysis of Edna O'Brien, published in 1990, begins to address the extent to which O'Brien's fiction reveals the socially constructed nature of 'femininity'. Salmon argues that 'the impossibility of a woman living as her authentic self in worlds ruled by men is *the* theme of O'Brien's fiction' (my italics).[26] This may be overstated, but Salmon identifies a crucial factor in O'Brien's fiction which was overlooked by early critics who condemned the perceived neglect of 'social institutions and ties', namely that 'woman' is isolated within social and symbolic orders constructed according to the masculine. Salmon's analysis places O'Brien's fiction within the context of de Beauvoir's identification of 'the masquerade', later redefined by Irigaray as 'mimesis', or the process through which 'femininity' is 'learned' through imitation of patriarchal ideals. Although Salmon does not cite Irigaray or Beauvoir, she points out that 'clothes as a metaphor for identity recur in all [O'Brien's] novels and stories' and that 'the characters wearing them know they are only theatrical substitutes for secure self-acceptance'.[27] 'Theatrical' is significant; Salmon's essay was published in the same year as Judith Butler's *Gender Trouble* which identifies gender as 'performance'. Post-1990, O'Brien's fiction – *House of Splendid Isolation* (1994), *Down by the River* (1996) and *Wild Decembers* (1999) – begins to concentrate on social and cultural constructions of 'masculinity' as well as 'femininity', maintaining her pace with the zeitgeist.

In 1996 the *Canadian Journal of Irish Studies* (*CJIS*) produced its *Special Edition on Edna O'Brien* which marked a turning point in criticism of her works. The eight essays in this collection cover a wide range of texts and theoretical perspectives. Maureen Grogan addresses the vexed issue of 'autobiography', comparing passages from the novel *A Pagan Place* and semi-autobiographical *Mother Ireland* in her analysis of narrative technique and authorial control. Identifying the 'disturbingly gender-biased nature' of much previous O'Brien criticism, Grogan sets out to question the labelling of her work as 'women's writing' by revealing the 'distance between the characters and their creator' and arguing that 'O'Brien's insights into the human condition transcend gender lines'.[28]

Rebecca Pelan – in my view the most astute commentator on O'Brien to date – follows her 1993 essay on O'Brien's 'stage-

Irishness' with an analysis of O'Brien's position in relation to James Joyce's partner, Nora Barnacle. Pelan begins by citing Philip Roth's much-quoted observation that:

> While Joyce in *Dubliners* and *Portrait of the Artist*, was the first Irish Catholic to make his experience and surroundings recognizable, 'the world of Nora Barnacle' had to wait for the fiction of Edna O'Brien.[29]

Pelan then analyses O'Brien's fiction within the context of this 'world' which, she argues, 'becomes symbolic of a post-independence Ireland in which women are material possessions'. Whilst Pelan's analysis is uncritical of O'Brien's problematic position in relation to Joyce – an issue which I shall address in discussions of *A Pagan Place*, *Night* and the Joyce biography – she does expose significant differences between their techniques.

Bonnie Lynn Davies and Lorna Rooks-Hughes offer French feminist analyses of O'Brien's fictions; Cixous's 'The Laugh of the Medusa' provides the theoretical framework for Davies's reading of the novel *Time and Tide* (1992), while Rooks-Hughes deploys Kristeva's theory of 'abjection' to reveal 'the challenges [O'Brien's protagonists] face in attempting to transcend or circumvent culturally sanctioned images . . . in contemporary Irish culture'.[30] It must of course be acknowledged that 'French feminism' is a problematic umbrella term encompassing theorists as diverse as Cixous, Kristeva, Irigaray and Moi, but their departures from Lacan all open up possibilities for analyses of O'Brien which transcend readings of her fiction as 'writing cure'.

The *CJIS Special Edition* concludes with Dawn Duncan's essay 'Edna O'Brien and Virginia'. This addresses not only the play *Virginia*, but O'Brien's strategic deployment of *écriture feminine* in *Night*. Duncan challenges the notion that O'Brien simply projects herself onto Woolf, arguing that, 'In *Virginia*, O'Brien creates a symbolic symphony of two feminine voices speaking distinctly but together of their struggle'.[31]

Yet, despite the *CJIS* milestone, traditions established by criticisms of O'Brien from the 1970s onwards die hard. In 1993 Kiera O'Hara's analysis of O'Brien's short stories expressed frustration with the recurrence of the 'love object' theme,

9

concluding that: 'The cycle of obsession – endless repetitions of yearning and despair – seems bound to continue'.[32] Worryingly, O'Hara's argument takes little account of the social, political and cultural contexts of O'Brien's work, and therefore misses the significance of O'Brien's concentration on compromised female subjectivity. As Rebecca Pelan astutely observes: 'That writers like O'Brien wr[i]te from marginalized social positions about women in similar positions is often given small consideration by a feminist criticism which too often assumes of female reality a homogeneity and ahistoricism which, by definition, also denies diversity and difference'.[33] Analyses such as O'Hara's ignore not only the context of O'Brien's Irishness – which will be addressed in the next chapter – but advances in cultural and women's studies such as Janice Radway's *Reading the Romance* (1986), an extensive survey of romance fiction and its readership which offers admirable insights into questions of genre and readership.[34] Studies such as Radway's offer valuable critical frameworks for analysis, rather than dismissal of O'Brien's perceived 'romantic masochism' and her protagonists' 'series of bondages to authoritarian and usually married men'.[35]

Whether or not we agree with Pelan's assertion that O'Brien's persona is 'not particularly endearing', this remains problematic.[36] Her charisma still threatens to preclude objective assessment of her work, and not just within the realm of media response. The *CJIS Special Edition*, which includes much incisive analysis, opens with the transcript of a somewhat sycophantic interview of O'Brien by Sandra Manoogian Pearce, who refers to the writer's ability to 'cast a spell over [an] audience'.[37] Rebecca Pelan argues that the crucial question in addressing the issue of persona is 'whether O'Brien, in setting out to exploit her Irishness, had other choices'.[38] This question will be examined, within the contexts of O'Brien's own Irishness and the 'Irelands' represented in her works, in the following chapter.

2

Edna O'Brien: 'Irish Woman Writer'

In chapter 1 I discussed the extent to which reviews of *House of Splendid Isolation* highlighted critical perceptions of O'Brien as an 'Irish woman writer' locked into the 1950s rural Ireland represented in *The Country Girls*. I pointed out that in her attempts to engage with issues relating to contemporary Ireland O'Brien exposed herself to dismissal as 'the Barbara Cartland of long-distance Republicanism'; political commentary sits uneasily with the 'colleen image' which continues to be imposed on O'Brien by reviewers and literary critics alike. This chapter will address the problematics of 'Irishness' and specifically of the label 'Irish woman writer', before suggesting readings of O'Brien which transcend these categories without dismissing their validity.

'Irishness' is especially problematic for the exiled writer – and it must be borne in mind that O'Brien has almost always worked as an exile. She has lived in London since 1959, the year before *The Country Girls* was published. In this sense O'Brien's perspective on Ireland has been consistently diasporic. A study by Gerry Smyth entitled 'Being Difficult: The Irish Writer in Britain' highlights the problems facing the diasporic Irish writer.[1] Smyth wrote a short story 'in response to a flier calling for fictional material articulating the experiences of Irish people living in England';[2] 'Being Difficult' records and analyses the ensuing correspondence between Smyth and the editor responsible for the flier. Smyth asks: 'For whom does the expatriate writer put fingers to keyboard? How is ethnic identity overdetermined by discourses of class, gender, sexuality, profession, and the myriad other factors bearing on the life of the migrant?'.[3] These questions are crucial to critical analyses of Edna O'Brien and her works. Chapter 1 identified some of the ways in which critical responses to O'Brien have been gender-specific. Smyth's study reveals the extent to which the 'English publisher' with whom he corresponded 'has . . . a particular kind of Mick in mind', that is, a writer 'who is concerned enough to realize his plight, but not "literary" enough to worry about the ways in which this plight can be represented'.[4] The editor in question was worried by Smyth's experimental narrative techniques, commenting, for example, on 'the intrusive narrator's voice' which supposedly got in the way of 'the omniscient third person', thereby compromising the perceived authenticity of 'the lives/experiences of Irish people living in England'. Subsequent chapters of this study will examine O'Brien's shifting narrative techniques in detail; for the moment, suffice to say that critics on the whole disliked her move from the seemingly subjective first-person narrative of *The Country Girls* to the more cynically detached double narrative of *Girls in their Married Bliss* (1964), and thence to *écriture feminine* in *A Pagan Place* (1970) and *Night* (1972) and the latest trilogy's specific engagement with issues relating to contemporary Ireland. Smyth's study suggests that critical resentment may have been at least partly generated by O'Brien's refusal to conform to 'particular kind of Mick' expectations. As Smyth points out:

'Being difficult' at a formal level – that is, problems of reference, allusion, intentional ambiguity, interpretation . . . raises the possibility of another way of 'being difficult' – either attractively . . . or dangerously so (the social Darwinism which construes the Irish as uncivilized interlopers).[5]

As I showed in chapter 1, continuing constructions of O'Brien as 'Celtic', exotic and sexually 'dangerous' have severely limited her status as a writer.

If 'being difficult' compromises the male Irish writer in exile, it poses additional, gender-specific problems for his female counterpart. Smyth points out the extent to which even Joyce 'is working within the limits of familiar discourses – the novel, the English language, [and] national identity'. Paradoxically, Joyce's attempts to evade these discourses have secured his continuing place in the academy and within 'an industry that has made a fetish out of difficulty'.[6] The problematics of O'Brien's own position in relation to Joyce will be discussed in the context of *A Pagan Place* and *Night*. For the moment, Patricia Boyle Haberstroh's analysis of contemporary Irish women poets highlights the Irish woman writer's construction by predecessors such as Joyce, Yeats and Kavanagh. Haberstroh comments astutely that 'Though all contemporary Irish poets have to face the Yeatsian legacy, women must confront issues not only of aesthetics but also of gender'.[7] Haberstroh cites Gloria Kline's critique of Yeats's attempts to define 'masculine' and 'feminine'; Kline comments that 'If [the woman] is herself an artist or a scholar, she must be so in terms of the masculine definition because no other exists. If she finds her identity in serving as the fixed center of things, then her intellectual activity, being 'masculine' in nature, is somehow exterior to herself'.[8] I shall return to this point later with specific reference to O'Brien's commentaries on female subjectivity, and on what Irigaray terms 'the masquerade' – the process by which woman constructs herself according to masculine definitions of 'femininity'. On a more empirical level, Haberstroh highlights the exclusion of Irish women writers from publishing circles, pointing out, for example, that:

> The recent publication of *The Field Day Anthology of Irish Writing* (1991) . . . has been severely criticised for sparse representation of writing by women. With no woman editors and little space devoted to women writers, this anthology calls attention to the continuing problems women have in getting their works published and recognized. Because such anthologies in effect create a canon, they will continue to perpetrate a vision of Irish writing dominated by male writers.[9]

Although, as Haberstroh points out, the *Field Day* situation has since been remedied, the issue of exclusion remains relevant to a writer who has been published since 1960. O'Brien's dilemma is, of course, one related not so much to the achievement of publication as to acceptance within the 'canon' created by institutions such as *Field Day*. Despite her prolific output,

13

The Country Girls is still one of the few examples of her work currently finding its way onto Irish Studies reading lists at undergraduate level within the academy. Despite Haberstroh's claim that 'In fiction, plot and setting allow writers like ... Edna O'Brien to imagine a world that does not demand the same kind of personal voice a lyric poem does', *The Country Girls* continues to exemplify for its Anglo-American readership a very 'particular kind of [female] Mick'.

In the context of women's writing there is a case for concentration on empiricism in the face of poststructuralism's deconstruction of the subject. This issue will be addressed in subsequent chapters. All too often, though, critical responses to accessible and apparently 'authentic' narratives are dismissive.

Certainly, critical and cultural responses to O'Brien's output exemplify the unenviable position of the Irish woman writer under review. Mary O'Connor argues, in line with Haberstroh, that:

> As women write, or try to publish, they define themselves (or not) as writers, and are encouraged to do so (or not) by society in various ways ... Women trying to publish in Ireland have a veritable hurdle-track of obstacles ahead of them: the fallen bodies of past women writers ... the received vision of self with its limiting idealisations and expectations; the ungenerosity of 'father figures' in the literary world to whom they have perhaps served apprenticeships; the implicit misogyny of mainstream publishing structures.[10]

Publishing in England and America has enabled O'Brien to sidestep some of these 'obstacles', yet her very success has proved in many ways to be something of a poisoned chalice. Patronage by Lord Weidenfeld has led to her marketing as a 'personality' and to relentless exposure of her private life.[11] Exile itself brings its own problems which will be addressed in depth in relation to *Mother Ireland* (1976), a text which explores the loss of 'mother country' from an overtly autobiographical perspective. Related to this are the absence of a 'literary mother' – an issue which I shall discuss in the context of the stage play *Virginia* (1980) – and O'Brien's ongoing construction as an inferior follower of Joyce. Furthermore, the Anglo-

14

American context of production renders O'Brien especially vulnerable to the 'particular kind of Mick' syndrome identified by Smyth.

In chapter 1 I addressed the issue of O'Brien's 'persona' and the extent to which concentration by the media on her extraordinary good looks has served to undermine her authorial status. In this chapter I wish to relate critical commentary and authorial persona specifically to Irishness, which is often perceived as one of O'Brien's major attractions. In an interview with Julia Carlson, O'Brien expressed her own irritation with this phenomenon, interrupting Carlson's assertion 'You were in a sense physically the image –' with:

> – of the colleen. Yes, yes. More codology, that sort of colleen image, being very pretty and unblemished, sitting at the hearth. Funnily enough, the so-called image makes a difference in England, too. I don't choose my own photographs for my cover; the publishers get a nice photograph because they want to; but again and again some snide remark crops up. That infuriates me. If you happen to have your hair done, well, then you can't be a 'serious' writer. It's so narrow, really.[12]

Fixation upon the 'colleen image' was especially evident throughout reviews of *House of Splendid Isolation* (1994), which as I explained in chapter 1 marked O'Brien's entry into the political arena. Concentration on the physical manifestations of O'Brien's Irishness paradoxically cast doubt upon her ability – or even right – to comment on 'the troubles'. Claudia Pattison's review affirmed that 'with her flame-red hair, milky skin and mesmerising green-flecked eyes, [O'Brien] is a bewitching Celtic beauty, even in her sixties'.[13] Ann Chisholm focused likewise on O'Brien's 'long greenish eyes, tumbled auburn hair, delicate bone structure [and] slender figure', though she could not resist adding that these 'have lasted well, possibly with a bit of help'.[14] Denis Staunton defines O'Brien's 'public image' as 'somewhere between Maud Gonne and Mata Hari'. The publication of *Wild Decembers* (1999) elicited an extraordinarily vitriolic response from Julie Burchill, who described O'Brien as 'rueful, wistful, shoulders drooping with regret and ennui ... carrying her emotional baggage under her eyes'. Burchill goes on to comment that 'even Miss O'Brien's hair is

15

not half as florid as her prose'.[15] Emer Kelly relates O'Brien's perceived 'wistful[ness]' specifically to her Irishness, commenting that:

> In Britain, her home for more than 30 years, she is seen – to put it somewhat cruelly – as a professional Irishwoman, her fey suffering girlishness to be admired as an enduring stance but never to be taken too seriously.[16]

Rebecca Pelan's focus on O'Brien's 'stage-Irish' persona places this within the context of 'the dominant discourses of Anglo-American literary criticism'. Pelan argues that:

> the authorial persona became the critical focus in direct correlation with the perception of O'Brien as a writer who challenged the dominant discourse by failing to confine her work within the parameters set for it.[17]

Pointing out O'Brien's 'uniqe[ness] in the tradition of Irish women's writing' Pelan identifies O'Brien's Southern Irish Catholic background and breakaway from the 'big house' tradition of writers such as Maria Edgeworth and Elizabeth Bowen as crucial factors in challenging dominant discourses. It seems that the more O'Brien's work is perceived as 'challenging', the more critics and reviewers insist on constructing her as 'a particular kind of Mick'. In the light of editorial response to Smyth's experiments with form, it is significant that Pelan attributes critical concentration on 'persona' to O'Brien's own experiments with form, genre and content. Pelan comments that:

> By 1967,[18] O'Brien was seen to have clearly shifted ground. No longer could she be comfortably classified or predicted in style or content. At the same time she was seen to have introduced an explicit political content at the expense of her former easy style.[19]

Critical response to O'Brien's unpredictability was to stereotype this as essentially 'wild' and Celtic, a tactic which was greatly facilitated by the banning of her books within Ireland.[20]

It may be helpful at this point to trace the literary and colonial origins of constructions not only of Irish women but of Ireland 'her'self as 'feminine'. I have already referred to Joyce and Yeats, and the extent to which their ideals keep the Irish woman writer locked into the position of imitator and/or muse. But these ideals are themselves historically grounded. O'Brien herself notes the multiplicity of feminizations of Ireland; her prose text *Mother Ireland* (1976) opens with the assertion that:

> Ireland has always been a woman, a womb, a cave, a cow, a Rosaleen, a sow, a bride, a harlot, and, of course, the gaunt Hag of Beare.[21]

In the context of the Irish woman writer's struggle for recognition, it is significant that Ailbhe Smyth analogizes feminizations of Ireland with patriarchal appropriation of language. Smyth's 'The Floozie in the Jacuzzi' is a response to the statue of Joyce's Anna Livia Plurabelle – his embodiment of the River Liffey – in Dublin's O'Connell Street, for which 'The Floozie . . .' is a colloquial name.[22] Smyth juxtaposes definitions of 'Irishism' and 'Woman' under the subheading 'CONSTRUCTIONS'. Analogies are made between the dictionary definition of 'Irishism' as, for example, 'equivocation', 'error', 'lapse' and constructions of women by Aristotle, Aquinas, Freud and Lacan as 'defect, lack, absence'.[23] 'The Floozie in the Jacuzzi' calls for the reappropriation and celebration of 'Anna Livia Plurability' as a signifier of the 'doubleness' or even multiplicity often associated with Irishness and exemplified in its negative aspect by perceptions of O'Brien as 'immaculately tousled'.

C. L. Innes offers an incisive analysis of feminizations of Ireland within the context of nineteenth-century colonialism, arguing that stereotypes of Irish womanhood derive principally from the colonizer's need to feminize Ireland and to construct 'her' as a damsel in distress who has to be rescued from her own people:

> Ireland['s] . . . salvation lies in her rescue and 'marriage' to her English father/husband, whose benevolent and patriarchal governance will allow her to fulfil her essential self and remain feminine and Celtic.[24]

This observation is deeply resonant in the light of the British media's obsessive focus upon the 'feminine and Celtic' qualities perceived in, and projected onto, O'Brien's writing and persona. This can be interpreted as a continuation of the colonial pattern through which 'Englishmen generally assumed their right as a "masculine and virile race" to control feminine and childlike races such as Celts'.[25]

Yet, as Innes goes on to point out, it is not only the English who are responsible for the construction and perpetation of stereotypes, since 'Irish nationalists and unionists even more frequently depict Ireland as a lady in distress'. Innes analyses the extent to which:

> Throughout the history of its colonization, Ireland has been represented by British imperialists as well as Irish nationalists and artists as female; she is Hibernia, Eire, Erin, Mother Ireland, the Poor Old Woman, the Shan Van Vocht, Cathleen ni Houlihan, the Dark Rosaleen.[26]

Ireland and by extension Irish women are thereby 'created . . . as the site of contestation'.[27]

Rebecca Pelan examines the implications of such representations for Irish woman themselves, identifying their continuing subjection to 'cultural imperialism' – the response of Irish men to colonization.[28] Innes identifies two principal 'cultural imperialist' stereotypes from within Ireland: 'those that depict Ireland as a maiden, and those that depict her as a mother'. O'Brien's fictions reveal the devastating practical implications of these representations. Innes cites Marina Warner's argument that 'there is a link between the assertion of patriarchal authority, on the one hand, and the apparent glorification of Mary, the mother of God, on the other.' Within these polarities 'biological functions' are denied, whilst 'motherhood [is proclaimed as] the ideal role for women'.[29] Innes outlines the similarities between 'Mother Church' and 'Mother Ireland', arguing that the 'two female images . . . both demanded the allegiance of men and women alike, but it was for women that they provided models of behaviour and identity'.[30] In terms of literature 'the figure of Erin and Mother Ireland' became widely influential, and 'the mother culture . . . provide[d] noble images and models such as . . . Deirdre' and the heroines of, for example, Synge and Yeats.

These 'images and models' have continuing repercussions for the Irish woman writer. Innes examines the extent to which 'the mythicization of Ireland itself as female may have influenced male writers in their choice of subjects [and] their perception and portrayal of Irish women'.[31] She points out that women 'in Irish literature and Irish history' have tended to be ignored 'except as muses or mates' such as Maud Gonne. Male authors such as Yeats undermined women's literary production and were hostile towards their involvement in political activity; again, these attitudes are discernible in reviews of O'Brien's overtly political *House of Splendid Isolation*.[32]

Innes suggests that Irish women writers' responses to cultural representations and practices have tended to be 'either to efface or play down their own personalities and identities as authors, or to allow their identities to be absorbed into symbolic constructs such as Erin'.[33] In the light of Gerry Smyth's 'Being Difficult' and of hostility towards O'Brien's experiments with narrative techniques, it is significant that Innes also identifies a corresponding tendency for Irish women writers to work 'within realist modes of fiction and drama'. Constructions of O'Brien as 'feminine' and 'Celtic' signify critical colonization of her persona and output. This in turn facilitates not only the safe containment of realist texts as ill-disguised autobiography, but the control of perceived narrative 'wildness' through hostility and repression.

Given the historical weight of literary and political constructions of Ireland as woman and of Irish women as 'muses and mates' it is difficult to envisage the issue of 'persona' as being anything other than problematic for O'Brien. Even Rebecca Pelan acknowledges the extent to which 'O'Brien's "Irishness" offered her for critics an obvious strategy for keeping the cultural and political contexts peripheral', despite arguing that:

> It would be futile to suggest that O'Brien has not contributed to the persona by romanticising and dramatising certain aspects of her life and personality, and by a manipulation of the physical presence to a level of often living out the role of heroine which accorded ... to a notion of nostalgic romanticism perceived as being typically Irish.[34]

Pelan later remarks that 'O'Brien's persona is not particularly endearing and has clearly worked to preclude her acceptance into Irish, British and feminist ranks of respectability'.[35] The

19

subjective nature of this response sits uneasily with Pelan's otherwise astute and objective argument. Nonetheless Pelan's point about O'Brien's exclusion from the feminist canon is vital.

I shall argue throughout this study that O'Brien's subversions of genre, narrative, and social and symbolic orders need to be re-examined. These are interrelated factors, as Gerry Smyth makes clear. Analysis of these factors is particularly relevant to texts from the late 1980s and 1990s which have not attracted a great deal of critical attention to date, and which explicitly challenge existing social and symbolic structures. *The High Road* (1988), for example, addresses a lesbian relationship in conjunction with environmental concerns.

A re-evaluation of O'Brien requires critical strategies which take into account issues such as constructions of 'femininity' and Irishness, the repercussions for the Irish woman/writer of colonialism, decolonization and 'cultural imperialism', and the woman writer's struggle to conceptualize 'mother country' without recourse to masculine definition. Cultural geographer Catherine Nash argues that:

> rather than simply assert the oppressive nature of images of feminized landscapes or women's bodies as terrain, it is necessary to engage with them to disrupt their authority and open up possibilities for difference, subversion, resistance and reappropriation . . .[36]

It is my aim in writing this study to demonstrate O'Brien's considerable facility for 'subversion, resistance and reappropriation'.

3

Negative Romance and Glacial Nihilism: The 1960s

As I suggested in chapter 1, Edna O'Brien continues to be defined largely according to her 'fey, charming and obviously autobiographical earlier works'.[1] Texts such as *The Country Girls* conform on the surface at least to Anglo-American notions of what is 'Celtic' and 'essential', whilst perceptions of the authorial persona have been shaped by the 1960s context of O'Brien's initial literary success. However, within the contexts of their production these 'fey and charming' texts are actually deeply subversive, offering radical deconstructions of 'femininity', 'Irishness' and contemporary sexual ideologies. I shall concentrate mainly on *The Country Girls* trilogy, referring also to *August is a Wicked Month* (1965), *Casualties of Peace* (1966) and the short story collection *The Love Object* (1968).

The Country Girls trilogy, comprising *The Country Girls* (1960), *Girl with Green Eyes*, initially published as *The Lonely Girl* (1962), and *Girls in their Married Bliss* (1964), is more 'obviously autobiographical' than *August is a Wicked Month* or *Casualties of Peace*. The trilogy charts the physical and psychic journeys of its romantically inclined protagonist Caithleen and her manipulative 'best friend' Baba from the rural west of Ireland to Dublin and thence to London.[2] *The Country Girls* and *Girl with Green Eyes* examine Cait's relationships with considerably older men, Mr Gentleman in *The Country Girls* and Eugene Gaillard in *Girl with Green Eyes*. *Girls in their Married Bliss* covers Cait's bitter divorce, Baba's loveless but financially astute marriage, and the extra-marital affairs of both. For anyone wishing to do so, it is easy enough to trace the 'autobiographical' elements of these texts from the Biographical Outline.

August is a Wicked Month and *Casualties of Peace* signify a departure from supposed 'autobiography'. In *August*, the displaced Irish protagonist Ellen leaves London for a holiday in the Mediterranean, where she experiences what Mary Salmon has termed 'a series of sad sexual encounters' and learns of the accidental death of her small son, who has been holidaying with her ex-husband. *Casualties* opens with its protagonist Willa's prophetic dream of being murdered; in a case of mistaken identity this is indeed to be her fate. After Willa's death her unconsummated marriage to a practised sadist is recounted through surviving letters. In this context it is unsurprising that O'Brien's own comment on perceptions of her work as autobiographical is: 'I'd be a goner now if I did everything I wrote'.[3]

Within the 1960s contexts of publication and production, though, the 'authenticity' identified by reviewers of *The Country Girls* is crucial to its ongoing popularity. Cait's quest for a national as well as for a gender identity was pertinent to 'a period when industrial expansion and technological development led to a substantial degree of geographical and social mobility, so that the bonds of community were loosening'.[4] Throughout her trilogy, O'Brien shifts the boundaries of geography, class and culture, yet her theme of compromised female subjectivity remains constant. As Bernice Schrank and Danine Farquharson remark of *The Love Object*: 'The central character in each [story] is female, and, despite differences of age, class and nationality, she is defined in terms of love'.[5] Only three years after the publication of *The Country Girls* and one year after *Girls in their Married Bliss*, Betty Friedan identified 'the problem that has no name', arguing that 'the core of the problem for women today is not sexual but a problem of identity'.[6] Friedan pointed out that 'a woman who is herself only a sexual object, lives finally in a world of objects, unable to touch in others the individual identity she lacks herself'.[7] In this condition, women are likely to enjoy reading fiction which itself explores 'loss of female identity'.[8] Furthermore, *August is a Wicked Month* and *Casualties of Peace* anticipate disillusionment with the 'permissive society' of the

1960s, in which, as Germaine Greer has recorded, it was 'not uncommon for a girl . . . to allow boys to take extraordinary liberties with her, while neither seeking nor deriving anything for herself'.[9] Similarly Sheila Macleod reflects that:

> Love had been largely a matter of sex: as much sex as you could get with as many people as possible. Now it seemed no more than a greedy male fantasy of omnipotence . . . Now the sixties looked very much like a male invention based in power, promiscuity and self-abuse.[10]

In the light of these retrospective analyses I would argue that O'Brien is remarkable not so much for preserving the 'fey' and 'charming' as for anticipating the zeitgeist.

As Rebecca Pelan points out, contemporary reviews of *The Country Girls* trilogy focused not so much on content as on style. This was 'consistently described as "fresh", "charming", "honest", "lyrical" and "uncluttered" '.[11] Likewise, in literary criticism, Peggy O'Brien nostalgically contrasts 'the ebullient *Country Girls*' with 'the glacial nihilism of the middle novels'.[12] Such perceptions fail either to acknowledge the subtext of *The Country Girls*'s perceived 'ebullience' or to recognize adolescent naivety as a necessary component of O'Brien's deconstructions of 'femininity' and 'romance'. Before discussing O'Brien's representations of Irishness in the 1960s texts, I shall examine these deconstructions through analysis of *The Country Girls* trilogy as 'negative romance'.

I use this term to indicate fiction which examines the condition of women under patriarchy by subverting 'romance' while conforming superficially to the genre. I feel that 'negative romance' more accurately describes *The Country Girls* trilogy than Janice Radway's term 'failed romance'; this identifies intended romance fiction which disappoints its readership. Radway's reader survey is, however, pertinent to O'Brien's early fiction. *The Country Girls* and *Girl with Green Eyes* are to a significant extent formulaic, perhaps most clearly so in O'Brien's delineation of Caithleen's lovers. Both Mr Gentleman and Eugene Gaillard are older than Caithleen, sexually experienced, professional, and rendered 'mysterious' by an inaccessible past life.[13] But O'Brien subverts 'romance' from this point onwards. In conventional romance fiction 'the power of men is adored, the qualities desired are age, power, detachment, the control of other people's welfare. And the novels rarely admit any criticism of this power'.[14] O'Brien's narrative techniques frequently 'admit criticism'; for example in *Girl with Green Eyes* Cait reveals that 'life with [Eugene] carried many rules which [she] resented slightly' (*GGE* 156). O'Brien's critique of masculine power is developed throughout the ironically titled *Girls in their Married Bliss*. In 'The Love Object' the narrative techniques through which Radway suggests that conventional romance fiction 'chronicle[s] not merely the events of a courtship but *what it feels like* to be the *object* of one' are partially subverted.[15] In this story the male is 'objectified' by the female narrator, who offers detailed descriptions of physical characteristics such as his 'religious smile' (which recalls the 'heros' of *The Country Girls* trilogy) (*LO* 147).[16] Yet there is always a danger that pastiche may not be immediately identified as such; this is 'the paradox of art forms that want to . . . speak for a culture from inside it and make it question its values and its self-constructing representations'.[17] O'Brien's subversion of 'romance' was missed by reviewers and critics alike; for example, her use of intertextuality was taken very much at face value. There are frequent references to *Rebecca* as Cait recounts the mysteries surrounding Eugene's first marriage, and Grace Eckley faithfully records that '[O'Brien's] home village of Scarriff . . . prompted an interest in literature through three books', *Rebecca* among them.[18] Assigning *Rebecca* to romance fiction, Eckley misses the point that Du Maurier too subverts the genre.

O'Brien's recurrent deployment of intertextuality emphasizes the socially constructed and intertextual nature of 'femininity' itself. Throughout *The Country Girls*, trilogy and – to a lesser extent – *August is a Wicked Month* and *Casualties of Peace*, varying levels of intertextuality, including references to 'Cinderella', *Rebecca*, *East Lynne* and *Wuthering Heights*, are instrumental to O'Brien's analysis of the compromised nature of female subjectivity.[19] In *The Second Sex*, published only eleven years before *The Country Girls*, Simone de Beauvoir revealed the extent to which 'femininity' is socially and culturally constructed, famously observing that: 'One is not born a woman, one becomes one'. *The Country Girls* show Cait and Baba in the process of 'becoming' women in social and symbolic orders constructed according to the masculine. The tensions inherent in this process are revealed in the following passage from *The Country Girls*, in which Cait is preparing for a date with Mr Gentleman:

> It is the only time when I am thankful for being a woman, that time of evening, when I draw the curtains, take off my old clothes and prepare to go out. Minute by minute the excitement grows ... I hate being a woman. Vain and shallow and superficial ... But I am happy at that time of night ... I kissed myself in the mirror and ran out of the room, happy and hurried and suitably mad. (*CG* 171)

'Woman' is a role which Caithleen adopts whilst recognizing its shallowness and being conscious of the extent to which she is 'playing'. Narcissistically kissing herself in the mirror, Caithleen might be described in terms of the Lacanian mirror phase, theorized by later psychoanalytic critics as 'represent[ing] the acquisition of femininity whereby the image of the feminine woman is mirrored back to the emerging female subject'.[20]

The extent to which Caithleen complies in the construction of 'romance' and of her own 'imposed role' is revealed by O'Brien's deployment of the language and accoutrements of fairytale. Mr Gentleman is introduced by Caithleen as first-person narrator as 'a beautiful man who lived in the white house on the hill' with 'turret windows'. He is established as romantic hero with the revelation that 'his real name was Mr de [sic] Maurier'. His social status and 'distinguished' appearance do recall Maxim de Winter in *Rebecca*. Though the age difference is formulaic – Tania Modleski points out that 'the most typical plot of female Gothics ... is one in which the lover plays the "father" ' – O'Brien undermines 'romance' by exposing the gap between Caithleen's adolescent romanticism and the reality of Mr Gentleman's needs and expectations. Mr Gentleman's initial ploy is to be managingly paternal, telling Caithleen that 'men prefer to kiss young girls without lipstick' and ordering wine for her when she 'would have rather'd lemonade' (*CG* 62–3). He gives her a beribboned box of chocolates which he sees as an appropriate gift for an adolescent girl but which instead anticipates her disappointment with romantic love, of which chocolates are an abiding symbol:

> I took the chaff out of the bottom row . . . There were only a few sweets . . . all the rest was chaff. I thought of writing to the makers to complain . . . but in the end I didn't bother. (*CG* 67)

Romantic stereotype is undermined by O'Brien's imposition of rural realism. Even as Mr Gentleman whispers sweet nothings, farmers save hay, children eat apples on haycocks and 'a woman wearing wellingtons [drives] cows home to be milked'. Farmyard references recurrently highlight the tension between reality and romance. Caithleen's first kiss from Mr Gentleman is followed by a walk into town where 'there had been a turkey market that day' (*CG* 101). The day before Cait and Baba leave for Dublin, where Cait's affair is supposed to be consummated, there is 'a pig fair around the corner' (*CG* 129). More specifically, when Caithleen comes home from school for Christmas she contemplates writing Mr Gentleman 'a magnificent letter, most of which I'd copy out of *Wuthering Heights*' (*CG* 71). Conversely Mr Gentleman tells her that she has 'got plump', which reminds her unpleasantly 'of young chickens when they were being weighed for the market' (*CG* 98). The operation of the sexual exchange market is a recurrent theme in O'Brien's work. In *The Country Girls*, 'romance' is finally undermined when Caithleen and Mr Gentleman undress for each other in Dublin. His penis is analogized with 'a little black man on top of a collecting box that shook his head every time you put a coin in the box' – an image which simultaneously suggests otherness and transaction (*CG* 175). Though Caithleen remains susceptible to the idea of romantic love, she has begun to be miserably conscious of its effects, admitting: 'Mr Gentleman was but a shadow and yet it was this shadow I craved' (*CG* 183). In this respect, as well as in terms of age and appearance, this anticipates O'Brien's representation of Eugene Gaillard as 'Gothic'. Again, later feminist criticism is helpful in analysing O'Brien; in her critique of Gothic romance Tania Modleski, for example, identifies the 'shadow male', 'usually a kind, considerate, gentle male who turns out to be vicious, insane and/or murderous'.[21]

This image is repeated in chapter 1 of *Girl with Green Eyes*, in which Cait reflects that '[Mr Gentleman] was only a shadow now and I remembered him the way one remembers a nice dress that one has grown out of' (*GGE* 7). A lover, like a 'nice dress', is a necessary accoutrement of 'romance', a discourse which is tenaciously seductive. Recalling putting on perfume to go to a wine-tasting reception, Caithleen reflects that: 'the very name ashes-of-roses made me feel alluring' (*GGE* 10). It is significant that 'ashes-of-roses' is a corruption of 'attar of roses'; this suggests that 'romance' will inevitably burn itself out. Interestingly, Cait and Baba gatecrash the reception under the pretext of representing a fictitious magazine – ' "Woman's Night", Baba said' (*GGE* 11). This is a subversive act on more than one level. Arguing for 'romance reading' as 'a technique for survival' Alison Light argues that 'women's magazines . . . do at least prioritize women and their lives in a culture where they are usually absent or given second place'.[22]

Throughout *Girl with Green Eyes* Cait's desperate clinging to romance accelerates in direct proportion to her reluctant self-awareness, her dread of Eugene's disapproval and, related to these, her fear of sexuality. Her doubts are externalized through the *Rebecca* dimension of the novel; as Ann Barr Snitow points out, one of the functions of Gothic romance is to legitimize male bad behaviour for the female reader: 'it is pleasing to think that appearances are deceptive, that male coldness, absence, boredom, are not what they seem'.[23] The housekeeper – a rural Irish Mrs Danvers – talks incessantly about Eugene's absent wife, Laura, while Kate tries on Laura's wellingtons, which do not fit her. This is an effective forewarning of Kate's inability to adapt to Eugene's way of life.[24] A direct forewarning of Eugene's dark side is present in a portrait of him 'look[ing] sinister', anticipating Tania Modleski's outline of the process, in Gothic, through which 'the transformation [of feelings] is from love into fear' (*GGE* 55).[25] In chapter 9 of *Girls in their Married Bliss* it is revealed that 'what [Kate] knew as love was 'fear and sexual necessity' and that '[Eugene's] little dictatorship demanded a woman like her – weak, apologetic, agreeable' (*GMB* 97). *The Country Girls* trilogy does not offer even the qualified 'happy ending' of *Rebecca*. *Girl with Green Eyes* continues to deploy intertextuality

as a means of undermining Kate's increasingly fragile expectations of romance – Eugene's friend Simon refers to him as 'Old
Heathcliff' whilst Baba observes that 'he's thirty-five and he's
going bald' (*GGE* 135). Resenting Eugene's imposition of
'rules' Kate nonetheless persists in 'lov[ing] him too much' – a
strategy which, as Radway points out, is legitimized by
romance fiction and by the romance myth itself, which
'suggest[s] that the cruelty and indifference which the hero
exhibits towards the heroine . . . are really of no consequence
because they *actually* originated in love and affection'.[26] In
these terms 'loving too much' is projected as a worthwhile
investment which will eventually pay off. O'Brien exposes the
pointlessness of this exercise by continuing to highlight the gap
between reality and romance; Eugene's parting message to
Kate is that 'old men and young girls are all right in books but
not anywhere else' (*GGE* 200).

In *Girls in their Married Bliss* the fragmentation of Kate's
subjectivity is reinforced by O'Brien's deployment of split
narrative; Kate is relegated to the third person which is
alternated with first-person narrative by Baba. The latter has
been identified by Eckley as 'giv[ing] Miss O'Brien a "feminist" label', a comment attributable within the context of the
1960s to reflections such as 'The vote, I thought, means nothing
to women, we should be armed'.[27] In the opening chapter Baba
reveals that Kate and Eugene have reunited and are now
'married [and] dissatisfied', leaving the reader in little doubt
that 'bliss' will not be on the agenda (*GMB* 7). Baba compounds earlier impressions of Eugene as 'shadow male' by
describing him as 'looking like an advertisement for hemlock'
(*GMB* 41). Her own comment on romance is: 'If this is how
true love ends I'm glad I've never had the experience'
(*GMB* 53).

In contrast to Kate's doomed romanticism, Baba's decision to
marry Frank has been a commercial one. This is clear from the
outset; Baba reveals that after their first date 'he drove [her]
home and offered [her] money' (*GMB* 9). She freely admits that
'the only times [she] found marriage at all pleasing [were]
when [she] was handing out his money' (*GMB* 56). Unlike
Kate's marriage, which operates in terms of exchange whilst
being constructed as 'love', this relationship is stripped to its

basics. Recognizing Frank as 'a merchant at heart', Baba recognizes also his suitability as a marriage partner in a society founded on 'the market'.

But she too harbours romantic daydreams, expressing 'longings, for songs, cigarettes, dark bars ... nights out, life'. 'Romance' in the form of a lover, though, brings abandonment and unplanned pregnancy. A visit to a gynaecologist to confirm this precipitates a diatribe against man and God:

> I was thinking of women and all they have to put up with ... All this poking and probing and hurt. And not only when they go to the doctors but when they go to bed as brides with men that love them. Oh God, who does not exist, you hate women ... (*GMB* 118–19).

Baba's recognition of women's entrapment by a male construction of 'God' who 'does not exist' in their interests anticipates O'Brien's ongoing deconstructions of myths of femininity under Irish Catholicism. In Baba's terms men hurt women in the name of love, and she refuses to glamourize her affair with the term.

The trilogy ends with Kate being forced to review her notions of 'love' after an unsatisfactory one-night stand. Denied sexual fulfilment, she feels 'What a cheat. Especially when one had set out to get something for oneself' (*GMB* 150). Kate begins to equate commercialism with romance – to recognize 'the market'; she is self-parodying about her quest for 'the De-Luxe Love Affair' and is seen ironically juxtaposed with 'a[n advertising] sign of multi-coloured lettering ... flashing on and off guaranteeing bargains, perfection and total satisfaction' (*GMB* 152). As Radway points out, 'advertising's offer of happiness is nothing but a promise of vicarious experience' – like romantic love.[28] Recognizing the futility of 'romance' Kate 'eliminate[s] the risk of making the same mistake again', undergoing voluntary sterilization in a self-destructive act of resistance to 'femininity'.

When *August is a Wicked Month* was published the *Guardian* identified 'brilliant passages of grotesque sexual comedy'; reviewing *Casualties of Peace*, *Punch* was even more exuberant, claiming that 'for laying, loving, sheer high spirits ... there hasn't been a book like this one since the last Edna O'Brien'. It seems strange that two books encompassing between them the death of a child, venereal disease, sado-masochism and murder should have elicited such gleeful responses. As Peggy O'Brien suggests, lovers of *The Country Girls* may simply have gone into denial, ignoring O'Brien's 'darker face'.[29] In fact the 'glacial nihilism' which Peggy O'Brien identifies in these novels constitutes a logical development from the 'negative romance' of *The Country Girls* trilogy, charting a continuum of women's experiences in a male-dominated society. Both novels explore the extent to which the 'permissive society' of the 1960s commodified women. Ellen, the protagonist of *August is a Wicked Month*, is quick to recognize the operations of the sexual exchange market when she takes a holiday in the Mediterranean. Displayed on the beach alongside her fellow commodities, she realizes that she is not one of the 'perfection people' and that she might have to market herself accordingly (*AWM* 51). Her seduction of Bobby, a film star, apparently allows her to sell herself above 'her own category', but his value is considerably reduced by the revelation that VD has formed a part of their exchange.

Yet Ellen, like Kate before her, remains susceptible to 'romance'. Her Mediterranean hotel appears to her as 'a fairytale house to which she was returning as in a dream' and Bobby likens her to 'Cinderella or something' (*AWM* 44, 145). As in *The Country Girls*, romance is undercut by reality; 'fairytale prettiness' is offset by imagery of death and violence which anticipates *Casualties of Peace*. The mattresses on the beach – the sexual market-place – appear 'like corpses' (*AWM* 58). Tensions between romance and reality meet as Ellen eschews the hotel dance, fearful of rejection, which she envisages through the discourse of fairytale, 'fores[eeing] herself sitting by the wall, ignored, and the magic falling away from her like fake frosting or gold dust' (*AWM* 57). *August's* exposition of the nihilism of the 1960s 'jet set' is echoed in the short story 'Paradise', from *The Love Object*. This ironically titled tale charts the end of an affair between its protagonist and her wealthy lover. Writing to her mother from his Mediterranean villa, she reveals that the 'jet set' *'brand you as idiot if you are harmless. There are jungle laws'* (*LO* 230).[30] In *August* Ellen's learned 'femininity' is mirrored by a transvestite dancer, 'a man who had perfectly mimicked all the coquette of a woman' and whose performance makes Ellen feel 'cheated' and 'sick' (*AWM* 87). Ellen's disgust is elicited by her recognition of the dancer's 'mimicry'; the drag act is a painful reminder of the fragility of her own self-image. Ellen, too, is ultimately a male-constructed woman who enacts her role. As Judith Butler later points out, 'the acts by which gender is constituted bear similarities to performative acts within theatrical contexts'.[31]

Casualties of Peace recounts Willa's attempts to construct a core of self in the face of physical and psychological annihilation by her servant Tom, husband Herod, and lover Auro. Her fear of loss of self is expressed in her opening dream, in which she '[finds] herself without a key' and in her adherence to virginity (*CP* 8). As Irigaray subsequently argued 'virginity has become the object of commerce' on 'the market' and has therefore 'to be rethought as a woman's possession'.[32] In this context, Willa's virginity can be read as an act of resistance to 'the market'. However, Willa's adherence to the spiritual is externalized by the stained glass with which she works and by which she is recurrently defined. The fragile saints and martyrs prefigure her own martyrdom; she is erroneously murdered by Tom, having borrowed a coat from his estranged wife Patsy, the intended victim.[33]

Willa's lover Auro is a consumer masquerading as saviour. He lives with and has a child by another woman, Beryl, and during his involvement with Willa picks up a girl on her way to a party, significantly a 'sad little tatty "Airfix" Cinderella'. Once again the discourse of fairytale is deployed to expose 'romance' as 'commodity'. In this context it is worth drawing attention to the narrative structure of *Casualties of Peace* which undermines 'romance' even more brutally than the linear narrative of *August is a Wicked Month*. Opening with Willa's prophetic nightmare, the narrative recounts the (bleak enough) affairs of Willa and Patsy. After Willa's death the 'living nightmare of [Willa's] marriage' is exposed through her letters.[34] It is revealed that Willa has been imprisoned by Herod in a Swiss dungeon, and subjected to physical and psychological atrocities in the name of love. There is a narrative – though not a chronological – progression of male

31

cruelty from Auro through to Tom and Herod. The use of flashback has the shock value of legitimising Willa's fears and exposing the universality of patriarchal 'nihilism'; following on from the Gothic aspects of *The Country Girls* trilogy, O'Brien accentuates the fragility of the boundaries between sado-masochism and romantic love. In this context *The Country Girls* can be reassessed not as the 'promising' debut novel of a writer who subsequently failed to live up to expectations, but as the departure point for a sustained and coherent literary output.

Although O'Brien's fiction manages within the social and cultural contexts of the 1960s to transcend nationality, 'gender' and 'nation' are conceptually linked throughout her work. Rebecca Pelan argues astutely that: 'Stories such as ... *The Country Girls* trilogy, capture the sadness and disillusionment of women in Irish society while ... they explore the reasons for such disillusionment'.[35] The quest of O'Brien's protagonists for an Irish identity with which it is possible to be comfortable is analogous with the search for a heterosexual relationship which avoids 'sell-out' in terms of female subjectivity. Indeed, this analogy may explain the banning of *The Country Girls* in Ireland; O'Brien herself remarks: 'I betrayed Irish womanhood ... I betrayed my own community by writing about their world'.[36] Throughout *The Country Girls* political allusions serve as expressions of Cait's sexual displacement; references to nationalism crop up like ill omens at points in the text where Caithleen is trying to assert herself so that the boundaries between national and sexual colonization are blurred. Caith-leen's impoverished family have been unable to live in their ancestral 'big house' since it was burned by the Protestant Black and Tans. Her mother, Mrs Brady, complies in her subaltern role, maintaining that 'Protestants were cleaner [than Catholics] and more honest' (*CG* 25). This is concurrent with her subservience to her husband. In *Girl with Green Eyes* Caithleen is dragged home by a family posse after her father hears of her relationship with the married and foreign Eugene; at this point she learns of the death of her aunt's lover at the hands of the Black and Tans (*GGE* 86). Later she passes crosses at the roadside 'where someone had been killed for Ireland' (*GGE* 96). When she is eventually abandoned by Eugene, her father misguidedly praises her 'for being so loyal to [her] family and to [her] religion'; meanwhile she is registering graffiti proclaiming 'UP THE IRA' (*GGE* 197). The ambiguous nationalities of Eugene and his predecessor Mr Gentleman blur nationalist/unionist dichotomies, underscoring the doubly colonized position of the Irish Catholic female, subject to colonization and to social imperialism. Eugene's scorn for Ireland and appropriation of Englishness can be read as a necessary defence for his own Jewishness, identified by Cait's Cousin Andy who comments on the size of Eugene's nose and makes the clichéd complaint that 'They'll be running this bloody country soon' (*GGE* 135). Despite being a despised outsider, though, Eugene is still able to colonize Cait, anglicizing her name to 'Kate' on the grounds that 'Caithleen' is 'too Kiltartan' for his liking, and thereby transferring his contempt for Ireland – a country which he dismisses as 'ridiculous' – to her (*GGE* 32). In *Casualties of Peace* Herod, a German gentile who is a Jewish sympathizer and who strongly identifies with his uncle, a fiddler who 'sawed his right hand off rather than serve' the cause of nationalism, has no compunctions about torturing Irish Willa (*CP* 131).

In *Girl with Green Eyes* Eugene's ambivalent responses to Kate's Irishness signify her doubly jeopardized position, which O'Brien emphasizes throughout the trilogy by recording her construction as essential Irish heroine. In *The Country Girls*, Jack Holland the grocer refers to her as an 'Irish colleen' – the very image which, as I demonstrated in chapter 1, has plagued O'Brien herself. After her elopement with Eugene in *Girl with Green Eyes* she is likened to 'Lord Ullin's Daughter'; in the light of O'Brien's intertextuality it is significant that Caithleen and her successors are increasingly constructed according to the Irish literary canon.[37] The dual commodification of 'femininity' and 'Irishness' is most succinctly articulated by Eugene's comment 'that [she has] a face like the girl on the Irish pound note' (*GGE* 16). This explicitly constructs her as 'essential' Irish currency. Later Eugene's predatory friend 'Simon the poet' plagiarizes Joyce in an attempt to chat Kate up: 'Well, here you are, shining quietly behind a bushel of Wicklow bran' (*GGE* 166). Kate's recognition of plagiarism does not undermine the authority of the literary father in constructing Irish femininity.[38]

Kate's fragmented 'feminine' and 'Irish' identities collide spectacularly at the scene of her breakdown at the railway station in *Girls in their Married Bliss*. This takes place after Kate and Eugene have separated; she has tried vainly to effect a reconciliation. Eugene fails to respond, offering Kate only a reiteration of facts – 'It's eight degrees below freezing'. Kate resents this, observing to herself that: 'England was screaming with facts and statistics and not one person to supervise soup machines' (*GMB* 96) In the context of Kate's alienation as an Irish woman, it is interesting that Eugene's mania for 'facts' is associated with his assumed Englishness and with his inability to nurture. Kate's desire for communication leads her to step onto a talking weighing machine. This speaks – and it is likely that Kate imagines this – with an Irish accent:

> 'Eight stone, seven pounds', a rich, Irish country accent told her. She talked back to him. He was probably shy, thinking that she was making fun of him, as no doubt many people did. A grey cloth map on the school wall, long forgotten, rose before her eyes ... Ordinary places that she'd never visited and never wanted to visit but were now part of a fable summoned up by this now familiar voice. (*GMB* 99–100)

Kate finds temporary solace in the reconstruction of her childhood Ireland, identifying with a fantasized and disembodied Irishman who has, like her, become an object of mockery and scorn. But Kate is still being 'weighed up' by the male who passes judgement on the female body. In a desperate attempt to overcome her own displacement Kate evokes memories of childhood food: 'She thought that maybe he had goose ... with soft, oozy potato stuffing to which sweetbreads had been added' (*GMB* 100). Yet O'Brien makes it clear that Kate is clinging to a 'fable', an inaccurate version of 'long forgotten people'. This passage signifies the necessity for returning to and reassimilating childhood memory and 'fable' if the female subject is to reconcile the disparate elements of her fractured identity. Following on from the 'glacial nihilism' of the later 1960s texts, O'Brien seeks to realize cohesion in *A Pagan Place*, *Night* and *Virginia*.

4

'Woman Must Write Herself': *A Pagan Place* and *Night*

In 1972 Edna O'Brien wrote a column for *The Times* to coincide with the publication of her experimental novel *Night*. Acknowledging the influence of Virginia Woolf, this was titled 'A Reason of One's Own'. O'Brien begins by identifying the importance of the 'real debris that is on the unexplored rubbish heaps of childhood' within the context of:

> A life-style packed with banalities. Brittle nights out and then the hangover and a *resumé* of conversation all pickled with 'I' and 'my' and 'mine'.

This suggests continuing disaffection with the social nihilism exposed throughout the later 1960s texts, and a recognition of the need for the female subject to effect cohesion through the recovery of memory and myth – a strategy which informs *A Pagan Place* (1970) and *Night* (1972).

In chapter 2 I indicated that O'Brien's early critics and reviewers were receptive to her first-person, linear narratives, dissenting only when this mode was disrupted in *Girls in their Married Bliss*. I cited Gerry Smyth's commentary on responses to the exiled Irish writer as 'being difficult' – responses which tend to be generated by departure from 'confessional', 'authentic' narrative technique. In *A Pagan Place* and *Night* O'Brien begins 'being difficult' in earnest, experimenting with second-person narrative, *écriture feminine* and – developing techniques initially deployed in *Casualties of Peace* – complex temporal and spatial shifts.

I have already suggested that ' "being difficult" at a formal level' poses specific problems for the Irish woman writer working in the rearguard of literary 'fathers' such as Yeats and Joyce. These problems exist on a continuum of compromised female subjectivity along with 'woman's' struggle for access to the phallocratic symbolic order – which necessitates separation from the mother – and the problems peculiar to the Irish woman whose 'mother country' is appropriated by the masculine. Within these contexts 'French feminist' and ecofeminist critical frameworks become increasingly pertinent to O'Brien's texts, since we can legitimately argue that she anticipated them.[1]

The narrative techniques of 'A Reason of One's Own' significantly encapsulate those of the experimental texts. Recounting a dream of 'various relatives', O'Brien reveals: 'I was trying to escape'. The narrative then shifts to the second person: 'Your mother was sentenced to prison . . . You must do something . . .' The dream itself recalls Willa's nightmare in *Casualties of Peace*, whilst the second-person narrative echoes *A Pagan Place*, throughout which this voice is constant. It is as though the narrator is addressing a childhood gestalt, which 'grants the "I" its identity', providing 'an image of coherence' and 'permit[ting] the "I" to come together from fragmentary points, to gain some stability'.[2] In *Night*, the protagonist, Mary Hooligan, seeks to achieve cohesion of her own 'fragmentary points', devoting the titular 'night' to the assimilation of childhood and subsequent memories and experiences. Similarly, the opening directions of *Virginia* indicate that she should appear as a 'grown woman' and as her 'youthful self' (*V* 7). It is significant that narrative techniques such as second-person narrative and *écriture feminine* celebrate rather than marginalize compromised subjectivity, rejecting what Mary Daly has termed 'the "I" of phallocratic language'.[3] O'Brien's reclamation of childhood memory rejects also the 'banalities' of the (patriarchal) 'life-style' condemned in 'A Reason of One's Own'.

In 'The Laugh of the Medusa' Helen Cixous argues that 'Woman must write her self', 'put[ting] herself into the text – as into the world and into history – by her own movement'.[4] *A Pagan Place* develops *The Country Girls*' 'autobiographical' narrative, recounting the childhood and adolescence of its significantly nameless Irish female protagonist, who at the end of the novel enters a convent. Throughout this novel, form and content – O'Brien's 'own movement' – put 'Irish woman' not only 'into the text', but into a revisited and reconceptualized 'Ireland'. O'Brien's narrative experiments are significant in the light of C. L. Innes's argument – which I cited in chapter 2 – that through being 'locked into confrontation with Britain and contestation over the motherland, Irish literature and Irish history have created males as national subjects, women as the site of contestation'.[5] *A Pagan Place* and *Night* can be read as adaptations of 'marginalization' to O'Brien's own agenda, enabling the author to explore 'women as the site of contestation' through her exposition of male-dominated cultures and her quest for a female imaginary. According to Innes:

> [Not much attention has] been given to how the mythicization of Ireland herself as female may have influenced male writers in their choice of subjects, their perception and portrayal of Irish women, of male–female relations, and of the interaction between the writer and the audience.[6]

Innes goes on to ask 'how women themselves respond[ed] to those images' and whether 'they seek to modify them and use them in their own ways?'

Although Innes is working on a timescale of 1880–1935, her observations are telling in the context of O'Brien's relationship with Joyce, which renders her deployment of *écriture feminine* deeply problematic. Joyce has been identified as a principal exponent of *écriture feminine*, which means in practice that for the woman writer there is no narrative voice which is immune from colonization by the masculine.[7] At the same time, though, the phallocratic symbolic order is subverted by *écriture feminine*'s celebration of the female body. In the context of O'Brien's fiction it is significant that Cixous aligns the female 'imaginary' with the act of masturbation, identifying 'a world of searching, the elaboration of a knowledge, on the basis of a systematic experimentation with the bodily functions' and arguing that: 'This practice ... in particular as concerns masturbation, is prolonged or accompanied by a production of forms'.[8] In the fiction of Edna O'Brien the issue of masturbation as an act of resistance is first introduced in *Girls on their Married Bliss*, in which Baba reveals: 'There's lots of words like frustrate and masturbate that [Frank] doesn't understand' (*GMB* 113). In *A Pagan Place* the narrator claims space through masturbating in a room in her father's house (*PP* 39, 46). In *Night* suppression of masturbation is explicitly linked to deprivation of language and to market economy. Recalling a particularly soul-destroying sexual encounter, Mary Hooligan recalls that:

> I thought I would go home and masturbate, that was what I would do, but it was early ... The sales were on and there was fifty per cent off everything. (*N* 71)

Mary's decision to substitute shopping for masturbation highlights the compromised nature of her subjectivity by emphasizing her own status as a reduced 'commodity' and by showing her conforming to patriarchal expectation; women are assumed to express themselves through 'retail therapy' rather than through masturbation. Back in the narrative present Mary reflects:

> I wouldn't mind a visit from the Holy Ghost, the paraclete with his tongues of fire. I can't master languages ... (*N* 71)

Mary's association of masturbation with access to language is clear.

Given that *Night* was dismissed by one reviewer as 'one long act of public literary masturbation', O'Brien seems to have succeeded – at least according to Cixous's criteria – in revisiting and describing her childhood 'world'.[9] Though Rebecca Pelan has argued that the 'experimental technique [of *Night*] is identifiably Joycean' O'Brien's mode of *écriture féminine* seems closer to Cixous's, if only in the light of Margaret Whitford's distinction between 'speaking *like* a woman and speaking *as* a woman', a distinction which acknowledges 'not simply psychosexual positioning, but social positioning'.[10]

O'Brien herself argues persuasively that 'women's lot is harder anywhere, but an Irishwoman's lot is ten times harder', largely because 'many Irish women are still in fear and trembling of their men'.[11] Colonization of Southern Irish men has created social imperialism and the dual colonization of Irish women. Cheryl Herr argues that colonization – 'the oppression of invading forces' – has 'led [ultimately] to a certain neutralizing of sexuality [and] *écriture feminine* in Ireland', and O'Brien has identified the extent to which the Catholic church has kept women 'frozen – mute'.[12] Given the gender-specific nature of this 'frozen' state, the efforts of Joyce to effect a reversal cannot speak fully for Irish women.

Rebecca Pelan confronts Joyce's *écriture feminine* by citing Frank Tuohy's suggestion that: 'While Joyce . . . was the first Irish Catholic to make his experience and surroundings recognizable, "the world of Nora Barnacle" had to wait for the fiction of Edna O'Brien'.[13] Pelan argues that:

'The world of Nora Barnacle' becomes symbolic of a post-independence Ireland in which women are material possessions, whose ambitions are rarely allowed to go beyond getting a husband and making a home and whose identity is formed entirely by an enforced domestic role as wife and mother.[14]

O'Brien's evocation of this 'world' in *A Pagan Place* and *Night* recognizes the need to 'put woman into the text'.

In *A Pagan Place* 'woman', 'text' and 'world' are assimilated as the narrator, recalling a beating from her father, reflects:

Your body, like your brain, was crammed with incidents. It had to its credit a seduction and a flaying in one day . . . It had all the years of fondlings, and strokings, from [the father], from [the mother], cramps after the Saturday morning senna, your first sanitary towel, the way [the mother] engirdled you each night . . . (*PP* 202)

Similarly, 'writing', 'history' and the female body are semiotically linked by the narrator's discovery of her sister Emma's diary and sanitary towel under her pillow (*PP* 112).

As well as 'writing the body', *A Pagan Place* rewrites 'Ireland', reclaiming female space within landscapes historically defined by the masculine. O'Brien's narrators have to contend not only with Irish and English literary 'fathers' and their constructions of 'femininity' and 'Irishness', but with their blood fathers in a society in which male excesses are permitted, even admired. The *Pagan Place* narrator struggles between 'fathers'. Reciting 'I wandered lonely as a cloud', she is told 'For Christ's sake shut up' (*PP* 68). As in the 1960s texts, intertextuality highlights the fragmentation of female subjectivity. Emma's diary reveals some of the literary sources through which she constructs her self – *East Lynne, Dracula* and *Murder in the Red Barn*. *East Lynne* subverts the domestic idyll, as I suggested in chapter 3; the *Dracula* reference anticipates *Mother Ireland*, in which O'Brien analogizes Stoker's tale of the vampiric absentee landlord with colonization of the female body, and *Murder in the Red Barn* prefigures Emma's own history, relating Maria Marten's seduction and betrayal.

The narrator's father is himself melodramatic, appearing early in the narrative in satanic guise and threatening his wife with a pitchfork. The mother's obligation to go to his room for sex is termed 'an edict', conflating conjugal and religious laws. This is telling in the light of Irigaray's argument that patriarchy and Christianity 'are in part myths which . . . take themselves to be the only order possible'.[15] But, like myths of a feminized Ireland, they are pervasive, endowing the father with the authority to lash out and swear, and to remind his wife that 'he took her out of the bog and gave her status' (*PP* 67). He is dominant in social gatherings, and he invades space:

> He shaved on the kitchen table and [his wife] put saucers as protection over the milk, the butter and the sugar . . . In disposing of the lather he managed to strew blobs everywhere except in the small china bowl that she had given him for the purpose. (*PP* 131)

After the revelation of her pregnancy Emma fears that he is 'going to kill her', whilst the fearful narrator is beaten into an orgasm which 'should have been [her lover's] to witness' (*PP* 154, 200).[16] The association of paternal violence and sexuality anticipates the centrality of incest to *Down by the River* (1996). In *A Pagan Place* the father's rage is largely attributable to the violation of his 'property'. In terms of Irigaray's theory of 'the market', and of women as ' "products" used and exchanged by men' – passed from father to husband – Emma and her sister have subverted patriarchal economy by 'tak[ing] themselves to market on their own' and prior to marriage.[17]

A Pagan Place exposes male domination not only of the female body, but of geographical space. Landscapes are named and claimed by the masculine; the father's dead friend, Dan

Egan, has 'a tree named after him', whilst 'saints and scholars [have] lived' on the island where he is buried (*PP* 13). The island's history has been shaped by a comprehensive range of what Innes terms 'males as national subjects'. A doctor who kills himself drinking and driving gets 'a hurleyfield christened after him' (*PP* 28). The father is proprietorial towards places as well as towards women, 'burn[ing] the house sooner than let[ting] the Black and Tans occupy it as a barracks' (*PP* 15).

As in *Girl with Green Eyes* and *Casualties of Peace*, hints of Gothic externalize and legitimize the narrator's fears. Crows nest in the chimneys of the family home, and the mother's wardrobe door is 'always opening of its own accord as if there was something struggling to get out' (*PP* 66). Mary Jacobus has identified the wardrobe as 'a symbol for [Freud] of his mother's inside'; in this context O'Brien's recurrent references to wardrobes signify her desire to realize a maternal imaginary, a figure which I shall discuss more fully in relation to *Mother Ireland*.[18] The wardrobe is also of course the repository of clothes and therefore of 'femininity'. In *Night* the wardrobe becomes the specific site of the gestalt when the child Mary Hooligan 'mis-sees' herself in its 'blotched' mirrors in her search for unity with her mother and cohesion of her fragmented self (*N* 13).

The *Pagan Place* narrator seeks cohesion through the recollection of female space, which though unnamed is claimed by association. The onset of her first menstruation is, for example, indelibly associated with 'a roadside where [she] had gone to sit and see horses and caravans and animals file past as the travelling circus came to town' (*PP* 103). This carnivalesque scene powerfully suggests the potential for female *jouissance*. Similarly the narrator rejoices in a tree stump which becomes 'hers' through association and ritual:

> When you passed your throne you sat because that was for good luck. Every time you passed it you had to sit. Sometimes to avoid it you made a detour. It was a tree stump, a seat of happiness with briars round it. You had a place trampled down for your feet. Elsewhere the briars flourished, were its garland   (*PP* 57).

The narrator is a *jouissante* Sleeping Beauty among her briars, luxuriating in her sense of inviolate space. Yet – and this anticipates Mary Hooligan's bisexuality in *Night* – she is simultaneously the prince who overcomes the briars to get there. The narrator attempts likewise to appropriate the 'pagan place' of the title. This is a circular 'fort of dark trees' where 'Druids had their rites' and where the ground is 'shifty, a swamp where lilies bloomed' (*PP* 17). Although the narrator is 'afraid of Druids' – whom she aligns with the living threat of her father – and although (as Innes argues) 'Celtic heritage' has been largely appropriated by the masculine, leaving little room for the conceptualization of a female 'pagan place', the narrator does claim the fort as her own before leaving for the convent, 'mak[ing] a wish and fe[eling] a lily'.[19] It is interesting that the lily, traditionally a symbol of sexual purity, is 'felt' in a dark place; this suggests an awareness of 'the need for a religious representation of conception, birth, childhood, adolescence, the female festivals'.[20]

In this context the narrator's reclamation of the Druidic site parallels her attempts to feminize Christian ritual, initially with a schoolfriend:

> Before your first Holy Communion, Jewel and you practised receiving the Host. You received bits of paper from each other ... (*PP* 18)

The narrator later plays with male ritual, venturing 'inside the [communion] rails' although 'no woman was supposed to do that' (*PP* 186).

Issues of religious ritual and female space are conflated in the episodes involving the young priest who attempts to seduce the narrator. His work 'in the South Seas' locates him as an exotic 'other' – the narrator associates him with flowers and sugar cane – and he seems detached from paternal law.[21] The narrator's sexual responses are bound up with her notion of a feminized 'place' and religion:

> You thought how you would love to go to the tropics with him and see people who offered mangoes and sweet potatoes to the Virgin Mary instead of flowers or candles. (*PP* 189)

This offers an exciting alternative to 'the image of the Virgin as uniquely asexual, denying all biological functions' and whose apparent 'glorification' is but another manifestation of 'patriarchal authority'.[22] The tropical Virgin and her exotic fruits suggest a carnal mother and – by extension – potential freedom from orthodox 'femininity'.

But when the priest finally arranges a rendezvous the narrator is lost for words: 'You sang dumb' (*PP* 191). The inherent contradiction of 'singing dumb' signifies the narrator's contradictory responses to the priest, whose implicit promise of escape from paternal law is, of course, empty. The narrator confronts her sexuality only at the site of his: 'You could see yourself in the buckle of his belt, distorted and gulping, but nevertheless you' (*PP* 195). Self-(mis)recognition can occur only within the existing symbolic order. The buckle in which the narrator sees her gestalt becomes the locus of threat:

> When he opened his belt and you heard it clang on the table, you strained to sit up and you tried to impede him from opening his buttons because it was nakedness that you feared above all ... He was saying no and you were saying no but you were at cross purposes. (*PP* 196).

As he begins to masturbate the 'petrified' girl is deprived of *jouissance* as well as access to language: 'Never were you more incongruous, never were you more unneccessary'. In the context of fragmented subjectivity it is significant that O'Brien deploys intertextuality at this point in the narrative; asking God's forgiveness the priest makes it sound 'like a snowfall, snow over the land and a mantle over the shoulders of the people'.[23] The echo of Joyce acknowledges the inescapability of the literary 'father', while the image of all-encompassing snow underscores the pervasiveness of the priest's semen: 'The smell of it got in the back of your throat as if you had drank it which you hadn't'.

Paternal law governs not only sexuality and religion, but the mother–daughter relationship. The blood father is made uneasy by the bond between the narrator and her mother:

> you sat on her lap. You put your ear to the wall of her stomach and you could hear her insides ... Your father told you to get down out of there, to get down.

Anxious to reclaim his wife he

43

Put his hand under her chin and forced her face up, told her to smile, told her she was getting old, told her she had wrinkles, called her Mud, short for mother. (*PP* 32)

In contradiction of religious and cultural veneration of Mary, Mother of God the bodily mother is 'muddied' by ridicule and by what happens in her husband's room: 'Before she went across the landing she put tissue paper in her pussy' (*PP* 33). 'The law of the father' asserts itself even as mother and daughter share a symbiotic closeness in bed: 'The crucifix sometimes slipped out of her hand and fell in the warm bed between you' (*PP* 34–5).*

Paternal law is subverted by forbidden desire for the mother.[24] This manifests itself in the analogy of the mother's flesh with food: 'There were spare rolls of skin on her back. They were like blancmange, cold and wet and appetizing' (*PP* 154). But desire is foiled by the mother herself. The tensions generated by enforced separation surface in the very different accounts given by mother and daughter of pre-natal experience:

> In your mother you were safe . . . that was the nearest you ever were to any other human being. Between you and your mother there was only a membrance, wafer thin.
> Once you were one with her. She didn't like it. She told the woman with the hair like Mrs Simpson how she was sick and bilious all the time. (*PP* 33)

The reference to Mrs Simpson highlights the replacement, within the symbolic order, of symbiosis with 'femininity', whilst locating the mother–daughter relationship within historical, 'masculine' linear time.[25] Intra-uterine potential – a concept which O'Brien will continue to explore in *Mother Ireland* – can never be realized within a symbolic order which immobilizes mother and daughter between options of 'consuming and being consumed', or separating 'into two dead selves distanced from each other, with no ties binding them'.[26]

In *Night* Mary Hooligan tries, like the *Pagan Place* narrator, to effect the union of her culturally constructed self with the

---

*Though the narrator's reflections on her body (see *PP* 202, cited above) indicate that the nights spent with her mother are indelibly 'written on the body'.

'elsewhere', or that which escapes the 'function' of 'mimicry'.[27] O'Brien's deployment of *écriture feminine* highlights and parallels this quest; Dawn Duncan argues convincingly that on a formal level *Night* realizes 'not a race consciousness as Joyce attempts but a feminine consciousness as crafted out of the feminine mind of O'Brien as she follows the path of Woolf'.[28] But, though *Night* achieves the 'disruptive excess' which Irigaray sees as essential to women's writing, O'Brien is also 'being difficult' as an *Irish* woman writer. Mary Hooligan's name is the site of multiple subversions; as a bisexual lapsed Catholic, 'Mary' subverts institutionalized Mariolatry, whilst 'Hooligan ... plays not only on Caithleen ni Houlihan, the personification of Irish womanhood and nationhood, but its colloquial meaning of hoodlum or ruffian'.[29]

Night's linguistically dense opening addresses issues of female subjectivity, Irishness, maternity:

> One fine day in the middle of the night, two dead men got up to fight, two blind men looking on, two cripples running for a priest and two dummies shouting Hurry on. That's how it is. Topsy-turvy. Lit with blood, cloth wick and old membrane. Milestones, tombstones, whetstones and mirrors. Mirrors are not for seeing by, mirrors are for wondering at, and wondering into. (*N* 7)

The Joycean opening sentence acknowledges O'Brien's debt to her literary father whilst asserting that life is 'lit with blood, cloth wick and old membrance', imagery which anticipates the novel's concern with the maternal body. *Ecriture feminine* is partially reclaimed from Joyce. Mary's quest for access to language and the symbolic order is signified by her assertion that 'Mirrors are not for seeing by, mirrors are for wondering at, and wondering into'. The tenacity of family ties, and the problematics of separation from the mother, are reiterated; Mary protests: 'I do not wish to lie with my own kith and kin' – but she doesn't 'want to lie with anyone else's' (*N* 11).

Before subverting – even *in*verting – patriarchy Mary identifies and defines its manifestations, listing 'dead men', 'blind men', 'cripples', 'priests' and 'dummies' in her deconstruction of Irish masculinity: 'I've met them all, the cretins, the pilgrims, the scholars and the scaly-eyed bards prating and intoning for their bit of cunt' (*N* 8). It is significant that 'bards' are listed among this 'host of losers'; Mary later subverts Yeats, referring to a pair of 'unpropagating' swans at her home village, Coose, surely a corruption of 'Coole'.[30] This reverses Yeats's 'appropriation' of female mythic figures such as the Hag of Beare.[31]

Mary even professes indifference to the supreme authority: 'I lie with my God, I lie without my God'. Pelan detects here 'a degree of cynicism, disillusionment and indifference which is absent in Joyce'.[32] Yet Mary's narrative is disrupted by the discourse of Christianity – '*Nota bene* . . . Hosannah' – and it is unclear whether she is reclaiming, or simply acknowledging the inescapability of paternal law. *Night*, like *A Pagan Place*, bows to the influence of biological, as well as literary and religious, fathers. Identities are elided as Mary reflects on her own conception:

> The seed of my father I reach out to you, as you once did to me . . . Her [the mother's] buttocks, flaunched and ordinary, the slit, the slit of absurdity into which we chose to pass. The nearest we ever were. (*N* 15)

In the social and linguistic absence of a maternal imaginary, Mary, unable to achieve a relationship of recognition with her mother, aligns herself with the father, ridiculing the mother's vagina in 'masculine' terms.

Paternal law is revealed once more as governing geographical as well as female space. The accoutrements of Irish literary landscapes are deployed in subversion of Yeats – 'Coose' features 'tombs, tumuli [and] a round tower'. But Coose has been patriarchally appropriated, documented 'in the Norse books' (*N* 36). Coose is significantly the site at which issues of 'femininity' and 'Irishness' collide. Mary recalls a fair at Coose on a holy day, at which 'a glut of Snow Whites' compete in fancy dress with 'several little drummer boys, jockeys, Tessie O'Sheas and bauld Fenian men', all Irish stereotypes. Mary's own see-through costume attracts a falconer who attempts her seduction; in stitching her daughter's costume, Lil stitches her up sexually (*N* 36). The falconer echoes the *Pagan Place* priest in ejaculating outside Mary, this time over 'the limestone rocks, the town's beauty spot' (*N* 37).[33] Farce is undercut by his ejaculate 'getting into the fissures, either nourishing or nauseating the lichen, the sphagnum, the roots of the tree, and the various insects and night creatures that were reposing there'. Male orgasm may be brief but it manages nonetheless to appropriate space.

The falconer is instrumental to Mary's displacement from Ireland – she leaves fearing pregnancy and Lil's wrath. As Pelan points out, her emigration proves only 'that escape is impossible'; geographical exile parallels her exile from language and the symbolic order and – like Kate and Ellen before her – she exchanges one form of male domination for another. Her husband, the 'aristocratic' Dr Flaggler, recalls Eugene and Herod in his clinical detachment and desire to control.

Yet Mary continues to resist commodification and construction. Throughout the text her world of 'halcyon days, rings, ringlets, ashes of roses, shit, chantilly, high teas, drop scones, serge suits [and] binding attachments' forms a parallel universe to the male literary Ireland of 'tombs, tumuli, vaults, boulders, a round tower, turds, toadstools and bullocks' (*N* 7, 10). Her resistance begins with her reluctance 'to lie with [her] own kith and kin', which she offers as 'another blow for King James and for the green' (*N* 11). Interestingly, though, she goes on to state: 'I do not wish to lie with anyone else's kith and kin either. One for King Billy', thereby rejecting the two patriarchal cultures by which her country is defined. But constructions of 'Ireland' are pervasive; by dawn Mary is returning to a conventionally feminized Ireland: 'Oh my dark Rosaleen, do not sigh, do not weep' (*N* 121).[34] Unable to escape the confines of tradition, Mary has to be content with appropriating its forms.

Throughout *Night* the problematics of conceptualizing 'mother country' without recourse to patriarchal definition are paralleled with those of the mother–daughter relationship. Like *A Pagan Place, Night* explores the incompleteness of the protagonist's separation from the mother. Mary's responses to Lil vacillate between hostility and desire, and she is as constrained by 'blood' and 'old membrane' as she is by law. What Irigaray identifies as 'the debt to the mother' remains 'unpaid' since the only available model is the Oedipal one of hatred and rejection. As Irigaray argues:

The Oedipus complex states the law of the non-return of the daughter to the mother . . . It cuts her off from her beginnings, her conception, her genesis, her birth, her childhood.[35]

In the Oedipal context it is significant that *Night* parodies *Hamlet*. O'Brien is not so much acknowledging a literary father as asserting the mother's role in the formation of the female psyche.[36] Irigaray argues that the woman 'divided in two by the oedipus complex' is left 'wandering, a supplicant in relation to values she could not appropriate for herself'.[37] But Mary does attempt to 'appropriate' masculine values and constructions. Lil's ghost appears to Mary, 'rouged' and with 'a rosary swinging from her waist'. Her appearance as an overdressed old woman is redolent of farce rather than tragedy, suggesting that the daughter's loss of her mother is taken less seriously than the son's loss of the father. Yet comedy gives way to profundity as symbiosis is finally realized:

She arched, tilted and bowed her body so that she fitted exactly into mine, my tumescence and her curves, and it felt as if we were being welded together, or at least moulded together, like one of her legendary carragheen soufflés . . . (*N* 47).

But this very unity is threatening, revealing the mutually 'immobilizing' effect of the mother–daughter relationship.[38] Like O'Brien, Irigaray represents this relationship in terms of food: 'Once more you [mother] are assimilated into nourishment. We've disappeared into this act of eating each other'. Mary can construct her relationship with Lil only in terms of consumption and in relation to male authorship; the realization of symbiosis is qualified by Mary's statement that: 'She was not like Hamlet's father, coming back . . .' Ultimately *Night* reinforces the message that 'the female Oedipus complex is woman's entry into a system of values that is not hers'.[39] For the Irish woman writer *écriture feminine* is 'not hers' either; to speak '*as* a woman' is still to operate within the dominant discourse. In this context it is significant that O'Brien goes on to conceptualize 'mother country' and literary 'mother' through the media of autobiography and drama, in *Mother Ireland* and *Virginia*.

5

'Another Birth': *Mother Ireland* and *Virginia*

Mother Ireland was first published in 1976. Part autobiography and part travelogue, it addresses constructions of 'femininity' and 'Irishness', domination of woman and landscape, and the pain of separation from 'mother' and 'mother country'. *Mother Ireland* simultaneously celebrates and undercuts the iconographies of Ireland which its deceptively guileless narrative and photographs appear to reinforce.[1]

I commented in the last chapter on the significance of O'Brien's shift to the media of autobiography and drama in her attempt to conceptualize 'mother country' and literary 'mother' without recourse to masculine definition. If 'writing like a woman' is an option available to the male author, the woman 'writing as a woman' might as well look beyond *écriture féminine*. In the light of Judith Butler's identification of 'gender' as 'an identity instituted through a *stylized repetition of acts*', O'Brien's decision to 'put woman' not just 'into the text', but onto the stage, is not unrelated to issues of 'writing like . . .' and 'writing as . . .'.[2] In *Mother Ireland*, though, O'Brien's shift towards autobiography seemed to signal that she had stopped 'being difficult' and that, in response to damning reviews of the experimental texts, she had engaged in the production of an accessible and undemanding 'coffee-table' book about Ireland. Yet *Mother Ireland* is a complex and subversive text, characterized by the same narrative shifts and ambiguities deployed throughout *A Pagan Place* and *Night*. I would argue that these ambiguities and subversions can best be understood in the context of Toril Moi's argument that the fictional and autobiographical texts of a single author need to be read 'with and against each other in order to bring out their points of tension, contradictions and similarities'.[3]

This technique has been deployed to a certain extent by Maureen Grogan, who makes ingenious use of *Mother Ireland* to highlight the degree of authorial control which she identifies in the short stories.[4] Rightly pointing out that '[O'Brien] has often been accused of a damaging and self-defeating subjectivity' and that: 'There seems to be little consideration of the possibility that the emotional content of her work is a deliberate artistic choice, not simply an uncontrolled eruption of the writer's experience' Grogan compares episodes from *Mother Ireland* with selected short stories, arguing that 'O'Brien, although strongly reliant on the power of personal memory . . . does alter, rearrange, and create entirely new stories'.

Grogan's article is incisive and convincing; yet the assumption that the short stories reveal 'the deliberate mediating presence of an adult narrator looking back and reconstructing her experience' while *Mother Ireland* simply 'tells it how it was' is reductive and misleading.[5] In this respect Grogan falls into the trap of 'treating one text as the implicit meaning of another'.[6] Moi's methodology needs to be fully deployed so that 'points of tension, contradictions and similarities' between 'autobiography' and 'fiction' can be examined intertextually. Given the position of the Irish woman writer producing in the rearguard of her literary 'fathers', and subject to social and cultural imperialism, it must be recognized that:

> The words on the page, though they may appear free and improvised, are on hire. They are owned by a complicated and interwoven past of language, history, happenstance.[7]

These insights question – and even invalidate – the separation of 'autobiography' from 'fiction'. In *Mother Ireland*, O'Brien highlights the perceived gap between 'art' and 'life' in her recollection of 'Edna' reading *East Lynne* at the kitchen table[8]:

> Nothing could be further from reality. The topped egg had gone cold in its cup. There was a scum on the cocoa, a voice was saying 'Have you done your exercise' or 'Get that table cleared . . . You . . . thought all the more wrenchingly of poor Isobel and all she had to bear. (*MI* 81).

Yet O'Brien's devotion of an entire chapter to 'The books we read' acknowledges the contribution of fiction as well as 'reality' to the construction of the (female) subject. Indeed, as I suggested in previous chapters, *East Lynne*'s subversion of the domestic idyll is far from irrelevant to the 'reality' of family life in Southern Ireland. The limited role models suggested by *Mother Ireland*'s references to (for example) ballad, film and melodrama exemplify the position of Southern Irish women:

> Despite the literary glorification of women . . . the reality for many . . . particularly those in rural areas, was their systematic removal and exclusion from every aspect of public life, trapping them in a domestic sphere.[9]

Not surprisingly, the intertextuality of *Mother Ireland* highlights the female subject's struggle to evade patriarchal constructions of 'femininity'. The developing sexuality of 'Edna' is expressed through the discourse of the poetic 'male gaze':

> To see a nun's eyebrow was as wicked and as bewitching as Keats felt when he saw the ungloved hand of the woman he loved . . . (*MI* 100)

Issues surrounding sexuality and nationality are obliquely addressed in the account of the fascination 'Edna' experiences with *Dracula*, a stage version of which is performed by a travelling theatre company visiting her village. This account is telling in the light of Deane's post-colonial readings of Stoker; Deane argues that 'Gothic fiction is devoted to the question of ownership' and that *Dracula* is 'the story of an absentee landlord'.[10] The dream 'Edna' has of being a 'stand-in maiden' suggests a willingness to collude in the enactment of colonial oppressions and in her own commodification – the generic transformation of *Dracula* from novel to play highlights 'femininity' and 'Irishness' as performative acts.

Inevitably *Mother Ireland* points to the Irish female subject's construction by Yeats and Joyce, and to the woman writer's predefinition in their terms:

> Christmas was three Masses in one day . . . and, long before – but you did not know it – Christmas for James Joyce was the plum pudding and the brandy butter, and the happiness of a dinner table disrupted because one woman was religious and raged against Parnell the adulterer, taking issue with a guest. (*MI* 74)

51

Similarly, the narrator recounts the way in which the exiled 'Edna' 'walk[s] the London streets at four and think[s] of how Yeats predicted such a thing' (*MI* 38). The issue of how the Irish woman *writer* is constructed in the shadow of her literary fathers is addressed in 'Dublin's Fair City'; on the very day that she wins a literary competition 'Edna' visits Finn's Hotel, where 'Nora Barnacle had been a chambermaid when James Joyce was courting her', and where her own parents 'celebrated their wedding breakfast' (*MI* 137–8). Later a man who congratulates her on her prize says that 'he hope[s she is] not called Sheila or Moura or anything Ballyhooley like that' (*MI* 38). The nascent 'Edna O'Brien' is constructed not only through her implicit alignment with Joyce's muse but in terms of what is perceived as a tolerable version of 'Irishness' (it is not difficult to trace the source of Eugene's renaming of Caithleen in *Girl with Green Eyes*).

'Edna' is able to elude definition only by experimenting with different constructions of 'femininity'. By the end of chapter 5, 'A Convent', for example, 'Our Lady' is beginning, in the face of an awakening sexuality in 'Edna', to lose her allure as a role model:

> I looked at one of the many pictures of the Virgin Mary along the wall and realized that she no longer spoke to me as she used to when I was a child. The visions were waning.   (*MI* 107)

Religious 'visions' are replaced by the accoutrements of 'the masquerade', that is woman's enactment of male-constructed 'femininity'; deciding not to be a nun after all, 'Edna' models herself on a 'film star', acquiring 'a perm in [her] hair . . . an accordion pleated skirt . . . high heels, perfume and fur-backed gloves' (*MI* 108). She recognizes this as a rejection of *Irish* femininity: 'I distinctly heard W. B. Yeats calling to me . . . But I turned a deaf ear'. Yet 'Edna' continues to be constructed within an Irish literary framework. Recounting her elopement at the end of chapter 6, the narrator likens her to 'Lord Ullin's daughter, def[ying] family and friends' (*MI* 141).

Exile compounds the ongoing construction of 'Edna' in terms of 'Irishness', so that the entire retrospective narrative of *Mother Ireland* aligns 'Edna' with her mother country. Echoing the acknowledgements – which highlight the importance of

'The Country itself' – the title of chapter 1, 'The land itself', suggests that this is going to be a book about – a biography of – a country. Yet the story of 'Edna' is interwoven with travelogue and legend, so that she is implicitly identified throughout *Mother Ireland* with Irish landscape and history. Peggy O'Brien has argued somewhat irritably that O'Brien 'aligns her own persona with the great women of Ireland's past ... rob[bing them of their individuality' through 'egoism'.[11] I feel, though, that O'Brien's perceived reductivism is indicative not so much of authorial egocentrism as of the constraining nature of 'femininity' and 'Irishness'. In *Mother Ireland* O'Brien's construction of her country as a raped and pillaged female – the opening chapter, for example, refers to 'the violation of her body and soul' – reveals the extent to which feminizations of 'Ireland' have become representative of Irish women themselves. 'Irishness', 'mother' and 'mother country' are significantly conflated in O'Brien's reference to the 'trinity [or shamrock] of guilts' inherited by Irish children, comprising 'the guilt for Christ's passion and crucifixion, the guilt for the plundered land, and the furtive guilt for the mother frequently defiled by the insatiable father' (*MI* 32). The interdependence of religious guilt and socially sanctioned motherhood is revealed by 'a little framed prayer' which hung 'above the black range in the kitchen', and which O'Brien cites among influential texts such as *Little Women* and *East Lynne*:

> May the meals that I prepare
> Be seasoned from above
> With thy blessing and thy grace
> And most of all thy love. (*MI* 82)

Marina Warner has cited the 'Kitchen Prayer from Knock' – similar to 'May the meals ...' but even more explicit – as an illustration of the sanctifying of 'the hardships of Irish mothers in their kitchens':

> Lord of all pots and pans and things,
> Since I've not time to be a saint
> By doing lovely things
> Or watching late with Thee
> Or dreaming in the dawn light
> Or storming heaven's gates

Make me a saint by getting
Meals and washing up the plates.[12]

In *Mother Ireland*, O'Brien describes – with more than a hint of resistance – the food sanctioned by paternal law:

> The meals were the mashed potatoes referred to as pandy, potato bread or boxty, and a concoction of potatoes, onion and cabbage called colcannon. To eat them was pure penance ... There were blackberries glistening on the hedge but a glacé cherry was as precious as a jewel. There was porter cake or the treacle cake that one turned up one's nose at, but a shop cake, a swiss roll say, stale as rice paper, spoke of another world ... (*MI* 82)

Considering the 'penance' integral to the consumption of food produced within the father's house, it is significant that shop cakes are aligned with freedom and romance and – in *The High Road* (1988) – with the maternal body. It seems paradoxical that cakes baked by the mother and produce offered by '*Mother Ireland*' are rejected – though edicts such as 'May the meals ...' exemplify the hegemony of social imperialism, shop cakes and glacé cherries suggest the commercial exploitation of women under capitalism. In *Mother Ireland*, though, shop cakes signify liberation from social and symbolic orders in which the mother–daughter relationship is immobilized at least partly by the expectation that the mother will become 'a saint by getting Meals'. In this context, the daughter's refusal of the mother's food becomes an act of resistance to 'consuming and being consumed' within a relationship configured by the masculine.[13]

In *Mother Ireland* 'consuming and being consumed' is significantly linked with cultural paralysis. Chapter 1, 'The land itself', lulls the reader into a false sense of security with a lengthy account of Ireland's history and geography which reads at face value as guileless 'travelogue'. O'Brien's subversions are in fact multiple – for example, she includes 'herstory' through reference to a nineteenth-century Kerry nun's account of Ireland. The most tangible instance of O'Brien's 'being difficult' occurs, though, with a sudden shift in the narrative voice from third to second person. This begins directly to address the reader and to critique an assumed response to Ireland:

Romantic Ireland, quite dead, you say, when you are sitting down
to high tea in Athlone, imploded with drop scones, apple pie and
soda bread. (*MI* 33)

The reader/tourist is crushingly posited as the obtuse consumer of a nurturing *'Mother Ireland'* and of 'her' home baking.
The reference to 'Romantic Ireland' is itself derogatory, evok-
ing constructions of Ireland as 'damsel in distress'; O'Brien
specifically observes that 'People fall in love with Ireland' (*MI*
32). This is a dangerous construction; as Chaia Heller argues:
'The romantic fantasizes that the woman needs knightly
protection from predators instead of recognizing her desire for
social potency'.[14]

As I pointed out in chapter 2, the opening paragraph of *Mother
Ireland* acknowledges a range of constructions of Ireland as
woman, from damsel in distress to devouring mother. Significantly, these are specifically identified as having been 'told and
fabricated by men'. In this context, Cheryl Herr's analysis of
feminizations of Ireland offers valuable insights into O'Brien's
attempts to conceptualize 'mother country'. Herr deploys
geographical and conceptual 'Irelands' to argue that 'identifica-
tions of Ireland with woman . . . who compels young men to die
for her [such as the 'Hag of Beare']' stem from patriarchal fear –
common to colonizer and colonized – of what she terms the
arkhein. For Herr this is a 'conceptual space' related variously
but not definitively to Kristeva's semiotic, 'a (m)other tongue,
[and] the speaking of Luce Irigaray's "two lips" '.[15] Herr argues
that the *arkhein* has been suppressed within Ireland by 'a
prevailing refusal of official sanction for Ireland's female-
identified prehistory'. 'Feminine' landscape features such as
mounds and tumuli engender fear of the devouring mother, so
that matriarchy becomes frozen into 'the myth of Ireland as a
woman [which] motivates the endless sacrifice of her sons and
lovers'. In this context the woman writer's reclamation of the
diverse feminizations of 'Ireland' can be read as empowering.
O'Brien's deployment of multiple feminized 'Irelands' gestures
towards what Ailbhe Smyth terms 'ANNA LIVIA PLURABILITY/*The
Singular Diversities and Diverse Singularities of Irish Women'*.[16]

But just as *Mother Ireland* exposes the gap between social and
cultural constructions of femininity and maternity, and the

reality of (particularly Southern Irish) women's lives, it highlights the dislocation of conceptual, feminized 'Irelands' from
'the land itself'.This is not to say that O'Brien is entirely resistant
to 'romantic' constructions of Ireland; at times the written text
fully supports Bourke's picturesque range of tinkers, turf-cutters
and Dubliners, whose beautiful-but-doomed faces are featured
in soft focus while the corporation flats which they inhabit are
tactfully faded into the background. O'Brien's invective against
Ireland's infection by 'rabid materialism, jerry building, visual
barbarities and a cultural atrophy that goes all the way to the
brain' seems partially to pander to the reader/tourist's desire for
'romantic Ireland' (*MI* 33). Yet the text is much more complex
than this. 'Cultural atrophy' is significant in the light of Cheryl
Herr's identification of cultural 'neutralizing' and 'stilling'
within Ireland. Referring to Joyce's 'analysis of this social
systematizing of repression', Herr argues that:

> Tracing the sources and meanings of his pain, anger, exile, and
> dualism took Joyce ... back to the most obvious features of
> Ireland-as-body ... visually organizing large portions of Irish
> geography. (*MI* 7)

Like Joyce, O'Brien deploys 'Ireland-as-body' in her struggle to
come to terms with 'exile' and 'dualism', and with issues of
writing and the body. However, I would argue that O'Brien's
agenda in identifying and analysing 'Ireland -as -[female]-
body' is very different from Joyce's, in that O'Brien is concerned not only with conceptual 'Irelands' but with the
desecration of 'the land itself'. O'Brien's environmentalism is
best exemplified by the revelation that:

> Most Reverend Dr Lucey, Bishop of Cork, fears that the country is
> not in danger of pollution from the oil rigs of Bantry Bay but that
> there is much more to dirty the minds of the people and to pollute
> their souls in the books, papers and films circulating through
> Ireland. Elsewhere you read that in fact due to a faulty valve two
> thousand five hundred gallons of oil spilled into the sea and a local
> councillor tossed the matter aside saying it did no great damage
> and that the Lord was on their side ... (*MI* 34)

Though this passage is largely self-explanatory, it is worth
highlighting O'Brien's exposition of the subjection of 'Ireland-

as-body' to the law of the father (bishop, councillor and 'the Lord' Himself) – a position which mirrors that of the Southern Irish woman under patriarchy.[17] In the light of this connection, it is interesting to note that Irigaray uses metaphors of geography in her discussions of female sexuality, analysing the extent to which 'female sexuality has always been theorized within masculine parameters' and arguing that 'the geography of [woman's] pleasure is much more diversified . . . than is imagined'. Irigaray speculates on the revisions needed 'to revive a very ancient – intrauterine . . . [and] prehistoric – relation to the maternal' in place of Freudian theories of sexuality. She goes on to liken this process to excavation, arguing that 'one would have to dig very deep in order to find, beneath the traces of this civilization, this history, the vestiges of a more archaic civilization which could give some indication as to what woman's sexuality is all about'. [18]

Like Irigaray O'Brien highlights the need to re/discover a maternal imaginary; for O'Brien, though, this need is located within a specifially Irish context and related to the desire for a 'mother country' conceptualized by the feminine. When O'Brien constructs 'mother country' through metaphor and abstraction rather than through reference to 'Ireland-as-body', she addresses issues not only of geographical exile but of woman's exile from the symbolic order. *Mother Ireland* reveals that for the Irish woman writer, access to the symbolic order has to be negotiated twice over; O'Brien writes that:

> To be on an island makes you realise that it is going to be harder to escape and that it will involve another birth, a further breach of waters. (*MI* 45)

O'Brien's conflation of geographical exile and separation from the bodily mother is significant in the light of Mary Jacobus's argument that:

> The discovery that the mother does not have a phallus means that the subject can never return to the womb. Somehow the fact that the mother is not phallic means that the mother as mother is lost forever, that the mother as womb, homeland, source and grounding for the subject is irretrievably past. The subject is hence in a foreign land, alienated.[19]

Jacobus goes beyond simply identifying alienation, questioning

Freud's theory that 'Whenever a man dreams of a place or country and says to himself ... "this place is familiar to me, I've been here before", we may interpret the place as being his mother's ... body'. In practice this means that 'woman' and 'place' are equally subject to definition by the masculine. Jacobus's response is to ask: 'in what mythic place could we at once re-find the maternal body and re-member ourselves?' Like Irigaray, she calls for the establishment of 'a feminist myth of origins whose function ... is to "re-member us" '.[20] In psychoanalytic terms, the masculine appropriation of conceptual and geographical 'Mother Irelands' exacerbates the female subject's struggle for agency. In the conclusion to *Mother Ireland*, O'Brien writes:

> Ireland for me is moments of its history and geography ... a line from a Synge play, the whiff of night air, but Ireland insubstantial like the goddesses poets dream of, who lead them down into strange circles. (*MI* 144)

Here the unequivocal first-person narrative unites the adult narrator with 'Edna', her childhood gestalt. But though O'Brien as female subject achieves partial unity of her fractured self, she is unable to reconcile this with a coherent image of 'mother country'. Like Mary Hooligan, she is left with a second-hand, and male-defined muse. *Mother Ireland* concludes with the express desire to recapture – through exile and return – 'the radical innocence of the moment just before birth', a state which may be read in the contexts of Jacobus and Irigaray as one of potential, preceding patriarchal definition and control.

Given O'Brien's interest in realizing the maternal imaginary which 'radical innocence' represents, it is not surprising that she chose to work on Virginia Woolf. Her stage play *Virginia* was premièred in 1980, and published in 1981 by Woolf's own publishers, Hogarth Press. *Virginia* signifies the desire to conceptualize a literary 'mother'; I have already commented on O'Brien's ambivalent relationship to Yeats and Joyce, and it is significant that *Mother Ireland*, for all its attention to the maternal, is prefaced by an extract from Beckett's *Malone Dies*. Dawn Duncan comments that throughout *Virginia* 'two female voices' speak 'distinctly but together of their struggle', 'one giving birth to another who gives birth to the former yet again'.[21]

I have cited Duncan's assertion that O'Brien 'follows the path of Woolf', in relation to *A Pagan Place* and *Night*. The links between O'Brien and Woolf transcend their common deployment of 'stream of consciousness' narrative, though. Duncan identifies biographical commonalities, pointing out that: 'Like Woolf, Edna O'Brien also suffered separation from a self-sacrificing mother and a domineering father'.[22] Bearing in mind Moi's strategy for examining (auto)biography and text in relation to each other, *Virginia* can be read as an attempt to unite the fractured identities of two women writers. Duncan refers to 'their mutual thematic concerns', which as she argues are principally related to the female subject's struggle for agency. One aspect of this struggle which Duncan mentions only tangentially, but which is crucial to the context of *Mother Ireland*, is the question of 'woman' and national identity. Examining this question in relation to Woolf, Clare Hanson quotes Woolf's assertion in *Three Guineas* that:

> the outsider will say, in fact, as a woman I have no country. As a woman I want no country. As a woman my country is the whole world.[23]

Woolf's projected 'outsider' suggests, according to Hanson, that 'a marginal . . . position makes for a radically different understanding of national and cultural identity'. Hanson argues that:

> Woolf makes an unambiguous claim here for the difference in view of the outsider and/or the woman in relation to national identity. Because the woman is not interpellated as a subject within the plural 'we' of national identity, she, in turn, will not recognise such identity.[24]

Hanson goes on to cite Woolf's assertion that 'our country . . . through the greater part of its history has treated [woman] as a slave'. Significantly, O'Brien's 'Virginia' takes a similarly post-colonial view of oppression, commenting ironically on the exploits of 'Leonard' in Ceylon, 'governing natives, shooting tigers, hanging blacks' (*V* 20).

It is not difficult to identify parallels between Woolf's position and that of the Southern Irish woman, 'colonized of the post-colonized' in the words of Ailbhe Smyth. The contextual positions of O'Brien and Woolf are of course very different; Woolf wrote her pacifist text *Three Guineas* in 1938, in response to 'the Spanish Civil War and the threat of the Second World War', whilst the position of 'Edna O'Briens as exiled Irish writer conflates 'woman' and 'outsider'. The writers and their respective responses to issues of gender, race and class are historically and culturally located. But they do have aims in common; I shall concentrate upon the connections identified by O'Brien and Woolf between individual and collective – or, more specifically, national – identities, and, related to this, on their common investment in the disruption of linear time.

Dawn Duncan examines the question of individual (female) identity solely in psychoanalytic terms; this is convincing enough, but Hanson's argument that 'Woolf sees a continuity between the construction of individual, social and national identies' is more productive within the context of O'Brien's attempts to construct a 'national identity' in terms of a maternal imaginary. According to Hanson, Woolf recognizes these diverse identities as commonly 'founded on repression, exclusion and sacrifice' and shows that 'we [women] must begin here, at the centre, with our (dispersed) selves, if we are to hope to change the symbolic and political order'.[25] I would argue that this is a position shared by O'Brien, and one which has been entirely overlooked by critics who questioned her early novels' apparent lack of attention to 'social ties and institutions' (see chapter 1). Such criticism is interestingly noted in *Virginia* when the eponymous heroine anticipates her own critical assessment: 'The subject of her writing was the little world of people like herself, a small class, a dying class . . .' (*V* 52). The connection between individual and national identities is raised in the conclusion to *Mother Ireland*, where O'Brien's assertion that: 'Ireland is a state of mind as well as an actual country' begs the questions: whose 'state of mind'? Whose 'actual country'? The artificiality of divisions between individual and collective identities is exposed in *Virginia* when 'Virginia' ridicules 'Leonard': 'Thinking you can affect the destiny of nations you can't do anything for your wife' (*V* 27).

Individual and national identities are further connected in being subject to 'masculine', linear time. In chapter 4, in relation to *A Pagan Place* and O' Brien's ' "being difficult" at a formal level', I cited Ariel Salleh's argument that patriarchal 'property systems' 'supp[ress] the amniotic flow of lived time'. The concept of 'amniotic flow' can be related not only to *Mother Ireland*'s recurrent (re)birth metaphors for the recovery of a maternal imaginary, but to the treatment of Woolf's suicide by drowning in *Virginia*.[26] Woolf was herself concerned with time, space and 'being difficult'; as Hanson points out she 'interrupt[s] and confound[s] the progress of linear time' in 'constructing the history of a nation' in *Orlando*. The circular structure of *Virginia* unites multiple versions of 'O'Brien', 'Woolf' and their pre-existing texts.

I have already commented on the significance of the direction that '*Virginia* appears as a grown woman and also as her youthful self' (*V* 7). In the light of O'Brien's attempted cohesion of the fragmented female subject and evasion of linear time, it is significant that Leonard Woolf and Leslie Stephen (Woolf's father) are conflated as 'The Man', to be played by a single actor. Duncan sees this as a device which 'denies the individual power of the male' thereby ensuring that 'the women are given distinct characters'. Certainly it is possible to read the reduction of father and husband to the signifier 'Man' as a celebration of female identity. There is, though, a more sinister dimension to this device in that the interchangeability of 'Man' highlights 'the law of the father' – note the upper-case 'M' – and (in practical terms) the commonality of patriarchal domination to lives as diverse as O'Brien's and Woolf's. Indeed 'Virginia' herself asks her father: 'Does it [domination] spread to all other men. Men in conflict for the different parts of my body' (*V* 14). 'Different parts' suggests fragmentation which is compounded by the necessity for 'the masquerade': 'Virginia' reveals to 'Vita' that there is: 'Always some misery like suspenders to clip my wings of glory and good God I must buy a hat' (*V* 47). As in *Mother Ireland*, a maternal imaginary is projected as the escape route from existing constructions of 'femininity' and 'nationality'. Revealing that she has been 'crushed and cranked in the womb' by her father's 'important works', 'Virginia' nonetheless hints at intrauterine potential, beginning Act I, scene 1, with an account of her dream of drowning:

'I dreamt that I leant over the edge of the boat and fell down. I went under the sea; I have been dead and yet am now alive again ... [The] sleeper feels himself drawing towards the shores of life ... something tremendous about to happen'. (*V* 3)

The pulling of the narrative 'I' into third-person masculine signifies the struggle to evade the dominant discourse, but 'shores of life' and 'something tremendous about to happen' evoke once more the state of 'radical innocence' projected at the close of *Mother Ireland*. *Virginia* ends with its heroine looking into the waves which will drown her, repeating the lines 'I have been dead and yet am now alive again ...' (*V* 63). Merging her own identities with those of Woolf, O'Brien addresses throughout *Virginia* the need for social and symbolic orders constructed according to the feminine. In the context of patriarchal constructions of national and gender identities it is significant that O'Brien's next major novel, *The High Road*, written eight years after *Virginia*, continues to examine the theme 'the outsider and/or the woman' within the contexts of a lesbian relationship and a seemingly alien culture.

6

'An Other Landscape': *The High Road*

Edna O'Brien has commented: 'I don't think *The High Road* is realized. There are things in it that are O.K., but it's imperfect'. O'Brien does not expand on *The High Road*'s perceived 'imperfect[ion]'; she simply reiterates the point that it is 'not [her] favourite'.[1] O'Brien's dissatisfaction with *The High Road* is regrettable given that this novel offers an admirably focused and directive critique of the social and symbolic orders of the Western world. In this respect *The High Road* may be a victim of its own success; the closure suggests that the potential of 'the radical innocence of the moment just before birth' which O'Brien identified in *Mother Ireland* is unlikely to be realized.

The High Road, published in 1988, recounts the relocation of its ageing Irish – though London-based – protagonist Anna to the Mediterranean. Scarred by a prolonged and painful love affair which, as she reveals, 'consumed [her] middle years like a terrible wasting sickness', she falls in love with a local girl called Catalina (*HR* 9). This results in a passionate affair which is consummated only once, after which Catalina is murdered by her estranged husband, Juan. *The High Road*'s Mediterranean setting and lesbian focus are crucial to the convergence of recurrent O'Brien themes of female subjectivity, national identity and relationships between women in a succinct and disciplined narrative which examines in detail 'the imaginary and the symbolic of intra-uterine life'.[2] I shall begin this chapter by discussing O'Brien's critique of culture and its commodification of women, before moving on to analysis of *The High Road*'s radical exploration of alternative frames of reference.

The critical assessment of patriarchy and the nuclear family which is so readily discernible in O'Brien's earlier works is sharpened throughout *The High Road* into damning indictment. The nuclear family is sparingly but mercilessly represented in Chapter 6; as Anna enjoys an idyllic hotel breakfast and reflects on her projected new life, the presence of a German couple and their children at the next table is an unwelcome reminder of what she has escaped. The couple wear 'identical seersucker shorts', signifying the elision of their individual identities, and:

> Soon as he finished eating, the man lit a little thin cigar ...
> The woman went on eating with a steady joyless rhythm as
> he delivered a monologue, which I was glad not to under-
> stand. (*HR* 49)

'Joyless' suggests the extent to which the wife's *jouissance* – or, in the context of women's writing, female sexual pleasure – has been suppressed.[3] Anna, not 'understand[ing]' the husband's 'monologue', seems to position herself not just outside of the German language, but outside of patriarchal discourse. O'Brien's deconstruction of the nuclear family is compounded by the account of an English couple and their children, of whom it is revealed that: 'To the proud father, Fiona was a water nymph and to the proud mother, little Ernest had the making of a Hercules' (*HR* 59). From Anna's perspective the family structure is the framework within which the children learn their gender roles; Fiona flirts with her father, offering him the ice-cream which she herself has licked, and Ernest appropriates the biggest portion of strawberries, 'look[ing] like a little weasel' as he bends over his plate (*HR* 59). Chapter 6 also offers Anna's reflections on the relationship from which she has fled; it is suggested that her lover has been a powerful, married man. Anna's recollection of walking around the Albert Memorial and Hall during their breakup implies a critique of the patriarchal values which the structures represent:

> There was wet plywood around the base of the Albert Hall which
> meant that renovation was in progress, and that the cupids and
> angels at its perimeters were grimed in soot. (*HR* 56)

'Wet plywood' suggests the need for reconstruction, while the soiled 'cupids and angels' expose the downside of patriarchally sanctioned romantic love, hinting that this particular myth has had its day.

Male domination is explored not only within the context of the nuclear family but through reference to homosexuality and – in Irigarayan terms – 'between-men' economy. Irigaray argues that Western society operates within a homosexual framework, since the exchange of 'women, signs and commodities' takes place exclusively between men.[4] In *The High Road* this homosexual economy is most clearly represented by Anna's recollection and account of her friend Portia's marriage to Pirate, whose name signifies the hijacking of female subjectivity. Pirate 'fuck[s] [Portia's] Daddy before he fuck[s] her', and leaves her immediately after the wedding ceremony. Significantly Pirate comes from 'a family who got their filthy lucre from the slave trade in the West Indies'; this recalls *Virginia*'s alignment of male dominance with colonialism (*HR* 34). After Pirate's departure another homosexual – 'Julian "the Crimper" ' – tells her that there is some graffiti about her in a women's toilet in Kensington, specifically 'Portia Whitehead is a lousy fuck' (*HR* 33). This is a 'sign' about a 'commodity' for the information of other commodities and ultimately for the benefit of men.

Even the apparently liberated Catalina cannot elude patriarchal definition and control; this is highlighted, post-*Country Girls*, by the echo in 'Catalina' of 'Caithleen'. Catalina is signified by the flowers which she distributes around Anna's hotel; the *jouissant* and lifegiving quality of roses and 'sweetpeas like wet jewels' are undercut by the revelation that 'they all smel[l] of water' having 'been sprinkled at the market' (*HR* 48). Like Portia, Catalina and their predecessors, the flowers are neutralized by commerce and exchange. O'Brien's juxtapositioning of lifegiving imagery with reference to 'the market' is significant in the light of Irigaray's argument that 'the symbolic of intrauterine life' – to which O'Brien alludes at the end of *Mother Ireland* – can function as an antidote to 'the phallic cult' in which women are 'objects to be used by and exchanged by men'.[5] 'Exchange' between Anna and Catalina operates outside of the dominant discourse, since within that particular framework women are able to communicate only as rival objects. As Pat O'Connor puts it, rather more simply:

> The recognition of women's ability to enjoy themselves with other women obviously undermines a romantic love ideology which stresses that true pleasure is only possible in the arms of a man.[6]

In *The High Road*, issues of rivalry and commodification are addressed through Anna's uneasy relationships with fellow women tourists such as Portia and Iris. An afternoon around the hotel swimming pool recalls *August is a Wicked Month* and Ellen's intimidation by 'the perfection people'. Women less glamorous than the 'imperious' and desirably skeletal Iris are dismissed as 'nameless creatures, identifiable only as one with beauty spots, another with a mat of hair under the armpits' (*HR* 50). Iris herself assesses potential rivals with disparaging comments about 'their awful bellies, their hideous bikinis [and] their bags with their names plastered all over them' (*HR* 53). Even the woman-centred Catalina is aware of exchange value; claiming to reject sartorial 'finery' and refusing to collude in her own commodification, she nonetheless admits that she 'cleared two terraces to get [a] blouse' (*HR* 113).

Catalina and Anna are both inescapably commodified according to 'femininity' and 'nationality'. Catalina is constructed as a 'little tragedienne' or 'mountain Carmen' by a man who affirms that 'there is one in every village' (*HR* 77). She is thus predestined to meet her violent and vengeful counterpart, Juan. This sense of fixed identity and destiny is compounded by the Irish exile D'Arcy's reference in chapter 1 to 'Catalina stigmatist and saint'. He tells Anna 'with casual clairvoyance' to 'mark the name', and that Saint Catalina is 'the Beata whom Satan tempts with sugar' (*HR* 40). At the end of the novel an onlooker wails 'beata, beata' over Catalina's corpse. Catalina's commodification leads ultimately to her death; 'exchanged' by a violent father, she dies at the hand of her husband.

Less destructively, but not dissimilarly, Anna is constructed as essentially Celtic. In a recent study of Irish women writers, Christine St Peter claims with specific attention to *The High Road* that O'Brien demonstrates a 'tendency to essentialize the Irish and the Irish soul'.[7] This misses the point that O'Brien identifies the convergence of 'essential' 'femininity' and 'Irishness' as crucial to the commodification of her protagonist. D'Arcy, for example, refers to Anna as 'little Druidess', while a photographer who takes her portrait at the beginning of the novel asks her 'to look sad and . . . think of all those dirges of [her] native land'. This recalls Fergus Bourke's image of 'Mother Ireland'. Unsurprisingly the two women find themselves relating to each other principally within a male-constructed frame of reference. Recalling 'Edna' casting her Keatsian gaze upon the nun in *Mother Ireland*, Anna fantasizes about dressing Catalina up 'in a taffeta dress the colour of fuschia, tier after tier of it' – a construction which sounds suspiciously 'Spanish' (*HR* 263). In the absence of a coherent symbolic representation of love between women, Anna can think of Catalina only as feminized 'love object' or 'chevalier' biker (*HR* 84). Even as Catalina emerges from the feminized and fluid sea, she is described in terms of a male artist's creation: 'She was blue upon blue, a creature Picasso had painted' (*HR* 109).

The 'Picasso' reference is significant; as in – for example – *A Pagan Place* and *Mother Ireland*, intertextuality is deployed throughout *The High Road* as a means of exposing the widespread nature of patriarchal ideology and control. *The High Road* is a haunted text, resonant with echoes of its predecessors. Portia and Iris recall the glacial 'jet set' women of *August is a Wicked Month*, while Catalina's father closely resembles those in *The Country Girls*, *A Pagan Place* and *Night*. O'Brien's epigraphs suggest the tenacity of familial and religious bonds. The first is a 'curse':

> God that berreth the crone of thornes
> Distru the prud of womens hornes . . .

while the second is a 'hymn':

> Mother Mother I am coming
> Home to Jesus
> And to Thee . . .

'Curse' and 'hymn' highlight the interconnection of religion, family ties and violence, prefiguring Catalina's murder and suggesting that her culture is not so very different from Anna's. In this context it is worth noting Anna's relationship with D'Arcy, a fellow Irish exile much given to Joycean pastiche. Intertextually 'D'Arcy' refers ironically to *Pride and Prejudice*; in *The High Road*, D'Arcy's status as 'hero' is ambiguous. He is ultimately instrumental in saving Anna's life, but he simultaneously embodies the inescapability of patriarchal culture and discourse. O'Brien, like Austen, is forced ultimately to acknowledge that woman's route to salvation lies in acquiescence to the dominant order. Certainly D'Arcy is crucial to O'Brien's exposition of cultural commonality; her deployment of Joycean pastiche in his account of a fictitious elopement signifies ongoing disillusionment with this particular strand of *écriture feminine*. D'Arcy's pastiche of 'Jolls Joyce' – for whom he expresses intense admiration – reinforces his hatred of women. His references to Iris, with whom he claims to have eloped, are abusive:

> 'She tried all the winsome, wonsome ways the four winds had taught her ... She tossed her stumastelliacinous hair like the Duchess of Alba in her light gown spun of Sistine shimmer ...' (*HR* 128)

D'Arcy's impotence generates rage which in turn is channelled into nihilism; he 'consider[s] strangling Iris' and later 'murder crosse[s his] mind again' (*HR* 130–31).

The violence exemplified by individual men such as D'Arcy and Juan is paralleled by *The High Road*'s representations of Catholic iconography. The Mediterranean landscape is dominated by the Stations of the Cross, while the female congregation of the local chapel remind Anna of her mother. Given *Mother Ireland*'s attention to 'maternity' this highlights the inescapability for Anna of masculine definition and control. Anna is 'drawn' to the chapel itself: 'Inside [it] had that aura of gloom and theatricality that I could never resist, that uniting of blood and glitter' (*HR* 19). Caught between 'blood' and 'glitter', the local women communicate their litany in a significantly '*sub*-human drone' (my italics). The litany itself is to the idealized mother Mary, who is surrounded by and constructed in response to male violence. As Marina Warner argues '*machismo* ... is the sweet and gentle Virgin's other face'.[8] The plaster virgin in *The High Road* chapel is represented 'crushing the serpent rather demurely':

> Above her was the Sacred Heart, with spikes of gold streaking out from His heart, skewers of pain and beatitude. Two points of

> painted flame above Him made shadows on the arch, and looked
> exactly like the bloodied points of two butcher's knives. (*HR* 20)

Such iconography points to the universality of woman's
suffering, prefiguring once more the stabbing of Catalina who
is in her own way a 'stigmatist and saint' (*HR* 4). The 'gloom
and theatricality', 'blood and glitter' of the chapel recall *Mother
Ireland*'s account of the *Dracula* production and the association
of Gothic with 'the question of ownership'.[9]

The High Road further recalls *Mother Ireland* and *A Pagan
Place* in offering feminizations of religious – and specifically
Catholic – discourse. In the light of Irigaray's argument that in
Christianity – because Christ was born of Mary – 'the body and
blood that are ritually consumed are the body and blood of
women', Anna's recollection of witnessing a bullfight is
revealing.[10] Anna tells Catalina:

> I bled for an entire week, in sympathy, with either the bulls or the
> horses or the young picadors or the strutting daring matadors, or
> the whole ritual which by its spectacle, its terror and its gore
> brought to my mind too vividly Christ's bleeding wounds and the
> women I knew, including myself, as if Christ was woman and
> woman was Christ in the bloodied ventricles of herself. Man in
> woman and woman in man. (*HR* 58)

Here O'Brien highlights men as well as women and animals as
victims of social and symbolic orders in which the phallus and
'Christ's bleeding wounds' form the bases of 'nihilistic religion'.[11] The stigma of Anna's prolonged menstruation signifies
the martyrdom of Christ, prefiguring the death of Catalina
whose hair, 'glisten[ing]' under the moon and 'matted with
blood', is given to Anna by her grandmother as a relic and
reminder that 'to love one must learn to part with everything'
(*HR* 180). O'Brien's imagery does however reconcile the
masculine economy with its exploited 'others' – women, bulls
and a feminized Christ. Anna's vision of 'Christ [as] woman'
suggests a maternal imaginary in which woman need no
longer try 'to resemble, to copy, the one [God] who is [the
father's] representative'.[12]

Catalina herself is the antithesis of nihilistic religion. From
her timely knock on Anna's door, 'carrying a great bowl of
flowers' and preventing the older woman from overdosing on

sleeping pills, she signifies *jouissance*, 'fill[ing Anna's] mind with something other than death' (*HR* 45). When Anna wants to buy a picture of a madonna and child from the market, Catalina stops her: 'when she heard the price she dragged me away' (*HR* 79). The 'price' for women of the 'Madonna' construct has already been acknowledged in *A Pagan Place*, *Night* and *Mother Ireland*. Related to cultural ideals of maternity, Catalina's attitude towards family life seems a long way from the Ireland of Anna's childhood. Anna reflects that: '[Catalina] had no illusions about family love whether it was among people or beasts' (*HR* 116). Indeed, Catalina seems fully to articulate the ambivalence expressed towards family ties in, for example, *Night*, in which Mary complains that 'people cling to [her] like sloths' (*N* 27). As Anna rejects the local matriarchs by tacitly refusing to attend Mass, she 'believe[s] that [she is] defying [her] own mother who had pervaded and begrudged every moment of [her] sleeping and [her] waking life, persisting even after death' (*HR* 19). This recalls Lil's posthumous hold over Mary in *Night*. Anna's 'defiance' suggests openness to the new order which the Mediterranean landscape appears to offer. At the end of chapter 1 the sea is constructed as an alternative mother:

> a great, dark, recumbent wet mother; mother of creatures, animate and half-animate; mother of life and death, moon and star, mother of the unknown . . . (*HR* 20)

Matriarchal culture is further suggested by Catalina's stories of her grandmother, who is said to be a witch. Catalina 'add[s] sprigs of myrtle' to the flowers in Anna's room (*HR* 57). Significantly, myrtle was traditionally carried by the initiates of Demeter's temple at Eleusis, to mark Demeter's search for her lost daughter Persephone; the sexual encounter between Anna and Catalina constitutes a symbolic return to the womb and therefore a reunion of mother and daughter within an alternative symbolic order.[13] Catalina's grandmother 'keep[s] the evil one out' of Catalina's house 'with a hyssop branch':

> they believed in spells, in spirits, in incantation . . . Her grandmother had reared her, had told her many secrets and together they travelled back in time . . . (*HR* 117)

Catalina's 'magic' encompasses her tending of the earth:

> She would never leave the land, it was in her blood, it was in her veins. She talked of how she dug the earth in places where the plough could not reach . . . She is not with me, or rather she is with me and I am the witness to her excitement as she describes putting the seeds in and weeks later the first leaf, the first little nursling above the ground. (*HR* 82)

This passage emphasizes Catalina's affinity with the earth, which transcends the reach of the phallic plough. Yet the reference to the plough highlights what Irigaray terms 'the submission of "nature" to "labour" on the part of men'.[14] Anna as 'witness' constructs a picturesque image of Catalina which is not so far removed from that of her construction as 'senorita'. The women achieve agency only on their trip to the mountain, where the lore of the mother replaces the 'law of the father'. As they ascend Catalina 'pat[s] an olive tree as she might a friend'; the trees themselves are likened to 'bowed witches', recalling Catalina's grandmother and her matriarchal inheritance. Catalina expresses regret that 'since Chernobyl the thrushes of the world have been contaminated'. Although the only local repercussion seems to have been that 'hoteliers would no longer buy [thrushes] as delicacies for their guests', Catalina expresses a more global view, arguing that:

> in a way it was a good thing that the tragedy happened, it made people realise that the world was one planet, countries were not separate . . . but vast families joined by something far more important than creed, or politics, joined by nature; and answerable to one another. (*HR* 144)

Catalina combines a global perspective with a strong sense of bioregionalism, or what Cheney terms 'storied residence', 'the notion of a mythic, narrative . . . construction of self and community'.[15] Her 'heroine' is Gaia, 'the earth mother who even when she lost everything was not vanquished. Catalina's ecofeminism is perhaps most clearly signified by the 'quilt' which she makes for Anna from fire-warmed leaves. In her proposals for 'an ecofeminist peace politics' Karen Warren suggests the deployment of:

> feminist theory building on the metaphor of quilting . . . [because] the quilts (or patches) tell unique, individualized stories about the

71

quilters and the circumstances of their lives; they are candidate patches for a larger, global mosaic . . . [16]

In *The High Road* the women's exchange of song and stories completes Anna's own growing sense of 'storied residence'. Catalina asks Anna for 'an ancient story' from her 'own land'. Anna tells the story of Queen Medb; this represents an imaginative leap from the childhood recounted in *Mother Ireland* throughout which the 'strong' women of Ireland's past – Queen Medb among them – were not considered desirable role models. Anna's post-coital responses are significantly expressed in terms of landscape; she feels that their night was:

> something to carry within us . . . a constant, like one of those streams or rills that one hears when walking along a country road, but that one does not see, simply knows it to be there. (*HR* 158)

Yet this construction of the relationship is problematic. The sexual encounter on the mountain is ultimately a 'one-off', time out from patriarchy, and Anna's new-found awareness of intra-uterine potential operates out of sight and, as it were, beneath the dominant discourse. In the context of ecofeminism it is significant that Catalina is identified with Gaia. Patrick Murphy has asked: 'Can Gaia imagery actually serve to subvert patriarchy when it continues the tendency to sex-type the planet Earth as female?' Chaia Heller's response to this issue is to point out that such iconography supports and perpetuates patriarchal constructions of maternity and that ' "Mother Earth" and "Mother Gaia" reflect an idea of nature as the pure, all-giving woman for whom every ecologically minded knight should risk his life'.[17] No eco-knight appears to rescue Catalina because she is not the 'pure, ideal, all-giving' woman promoted through Gaia imagery, but a feisty bisexual adulteress. Although, as Linda Vance argues, matriarchal imagery can 'offer a state of possibility, a sense that what might have been might also yet be' – a 'state' paralleled by that of pre-natal potential identified in *Mother Ireland* – such imagery ultimately ' "justifies" women's compulsory heterosexuality, motherhood, and submissiveness'.[18]

The problematics of Gaia imagery are matched by those inherent in *The High Road*'s recurrent metaphors of fluidity. As I argued at the beginning of this chapter O'Brien's use of such imagery is confused; this is not surprising given its ambivalence within 'French' feminist contexts. Throughout *The High Road* O'Brien continues to highlight the distinctions between male and female fluids which she identifies in *A Pagan Place* and *Night*, where semen and male urine are deployed in the appropriation of territory (by the priest, falconer and narrator's father) while female fluids – vaginal secretions and menstrual blood – are perceived as messy and a cause for shame. As de Beauvoir remarked in *The Second Sex*, during sexual arousal 'man "gets stiff", but woman "gets wet"', invoking 'childhood memories of bed-wetting, of guilty and involuntary yielding to the need to urinate'.[19] In *The High Road* O'Brien hints at the extent to which 'male' fluids are idealized and employed for specific purposes of acquisition and control, while 'female' fluids, including the feminized sea, are 'unstable' and beyond control.[20] In chapter 6, for example, the tourist couple's children Ernest and Fiona are characterized by metaphors of fluidity. Fiona is constructed as 'water nymph' while Ernest's bodily fluid is already being used to establish ownership – he trails spittle on his bowl of strawberries to deter anyone else from eating them. 'Female' fluid is shown to have its more sinister side though – a little boy's death by drowning in the hotel swimming pool echoes the death of Mrs Brady in *The Country Girls*, suggesting the 'unstable' nature of amniotic fluid in the existing social and symbolic orders. This also pre-empts *Time and Tide* (1992), a novel based on the death of the protagonist's son in a Thames ferry disaster. The very different death of 'Virginia' can be read as a compensatory celebration of female fluidity.

Tensions between images of fluidity as lethal or lifegiving (as in *Virginia* and *Mother Ireland*, where the regenerative potential of fluidity is explored) are matched by inconsistencies in O'Brien's gendering of fluid, specifically the sea. *The High Road*'s title is significant in the retrospective light of O'Brien's short story 'The Mouth of the Cave', another lesbian text. In this story the protagonist encounters a girl who becomes an object of unfulfilled desire. The encounter is a result of the protagonist/narrator taking one of 'two routes to the village', 'the rougher one, to be beside the mountain rather than the sea'(*FH* 173–6). After a fruitless wait for the girl, she begins to avoid the mountain road altogether, revealing that 'she always find[s her]self taking the sea road, even though [she] most desperately desire[s] to go the other way'. As in *The High Road*, the mountain represents alternative possibilities, 'time out' from patriarchal control. But surely, in the context of *The High Road*'s construction of the sea as 'great, wet, recumbent mother', it would make more sense for this to be analogized with lesbian sexuality? The key to O'Brien's seeming inconsistency may well lie in James Joyce and his use of 'sea' metaphor. Discussing Anna Livia – Joyce's feminization of the river Liffey – O'Brien recounts how 'she' 'returns to her first abode, her "cold mad feary father" the waiting sea'(*JJ* 143). Clearly Joyce's construction of the sea as 'father' and – in O'Brien's terms – 'first abode' echoes his deployment of *écriture feminine*, creating difficulties for O'Brien as she attempts to configure a maternal symbolic through images of fluidity. Though it is possible to reclaim such imagery, O'Brien's 'wet mother' may be overshadowed by Joyce's canonized and therefore in Irigarayan terms 'stable' 'father'. Furthermore there are similarities between the *High Road* sea and Lil in *Night*; there is more than a suggestion of the 'devouring mother' in O'Brien's representation.

The problematics of representation are best summarized in this context by Elizabeth Berg's discussion of Irigaray's use of metaphor. Berg explains that:

> For Irigaray, if woman is given an image – if she is represented – this representation must necessarily take place within the context of a phallocentric system of representation – Thus the feminist theorist is caught in a double bind; whether she presents an image of woman or not, she continues the effacement of woman as Other . . . The images [Irigaray] proposes – of fluids, caves, etc. – are empty ones.[21]

'Feminist theorist' extends of course to O'Brien as 'woman writer'. Like Irigaray's proposed images, 'The Mouth of the Cave' as vaginal entrance and sex between Anna and Catalina as a return to 'wandering milky watery bliss' are ultimately 'empty', constituting a temporary space outside of the dominant discourse rather than the realization of a maternal imaginary. On a 'grassroots' rather than a metaphorical level

Irigaray is acutely aware of this dilemma, arguing that contemporary lesbian relationships actually parallel the existing 'between-men' economy, thereby 'do[ing] far less to upset existing institutions and dogmas than would a real change in the respective status of the female and male genders'.[22] By the end of *The High Road* O'Brien too shows that 'being outside the symbolic order is not a condition to which women should aspire [because] the absence of adequate symbolization is the dereliction in which they already exist'.[23] The 1990s trilogy which I shall discuss in the following chapter acknowledges the need for direct engagement with the dominant discourse as a means towards the realization of social and symbolic reform.

7

'Might Before Right': The 1990s Trilogy

In 1985, three years before the publication of *The High Road*, O'Brien was asked: '... considering your emotional involvement with Ireland, how have you kept away from the situation in Northern Ireland – terrorism, the IRA, etc. ...?' O'Brien's response was:

> I have not set a novel in Northern Ireland simply because I do not know enough about it. I dislike cant – you get that from politicians. Writers have to dig deep for experience ... so far I have refrained from bringing the topic into a book merely as a voyeur.[1]

House of Splendid Isolation – a novel set in Southern Ireland but taking as its male protagonist a republican fugitive from the north – was published nine years later. As I noted in chapter 2, critics were ambivalent about O'Brien's engagement with 'the troubles'.

Sophia Hillan King has recently contested the view that O'Brien's engagement with 'the IRA, abortion and land ... [has] ... seen her castigated as out of touch with modern Ireland'. King argues that 'Perhaps the opposite is true: it may prove to be the case that Edna O'Brien is utterly in touch', since 'it seems that the sectarian violence, sexual repression, and what used to be called "the land question" are still central to Irish life'.[2] O'Brien is still attuned to the zeitgeist.

Following *The High Road*'s revelation of woman's 'state of dereliction outside the symbolic order', the trilogy's engagement with terrorism, incestuous rape, abortion and land ownership offers considerable scope for O'Brien's ongoing analysis of 'women in society'.[3] *House of Splendid Isolation* (1994) recounts its elderly protagonist's relationship with a republican on the run who shelters in her 'big house' in the south; *Down by the River*'s 14-year-old protagonist is raped and made pregnant by her father (1996), and in *Wild Decembers* (1999) the protagonist's lover is shot by her brother in a dispute over land. O'Brien's exposition of patriarchal nihilism is familiar, but the novels of the 1990s represent a significant departure from their predecessors. Whilst the earlier works concentrate 'femininity' and woman's exclusion from social and symbolic orders, the latest trilogy deconstructs 'masculinity' as well as 'femininity'. Gone are the two-dimensional 'shadow-males' of *Girls in their Married Bliss* and *Casulaties of Peace*; instead a comprehensive range of what Innes terms 'males as national subjects' are examined as socially constructed and sentient beings. In *House of Splendid Isolation*, for example, O'Brien offers Rory the guard's perspective on marriage:

> 'You live in clover', he says [to his wife] and gestures to a new carpet, the cuckoo clock, the sideboard crammed with ornaments ... Wardrobes. Finery. Jewellery. Lolly. There was a time when this avarice of hers was a charm in itself and never did he go for a trip or do a job without bringing back some little thing to hang on her. (*HSI* 10)

Here the gradual attrition of 'romance' is not simply implied but clearly delineated from a male point of view.[4] Sheila has been constructed as 'consumer' and defined by her possessions, and Rory has become disenchanted with the very qualities which initially defined her as 'feminine'; he loses out through colluding in her commodification.

In *Down by the River*, O'Brien attempts to render her protagonist's father James Macnamara understandable if not actually sympathetic. As James is faced with prosecution he contemplates – and subsequently commits – suicide. O'Brien is careful to construct him throughout this process as a sentient being, offering insight into his state of mind:

> When did it start. Why did it start. His blood about to be dispatched to Oxford to undergo a test. Why did it start. Why did it start. Who in the whole world could answer that for him when he himself did not know. (*DR* 249)

James, whose motto is 'might before right' and who significantly measures his land before raping his daughter, exemplifies the way in which:

> colonised peoples . . . tend to observe or impose strictly differentiated gender roles in order to assert the masculinity and right to power of the (male) subject.[5]

O'Brien's detailed characterizations of men typify her attempts throughout *House of Splendid Isolation* to place the issues examined in previous texts within their broader socio-political contexts. In *House of Splendid Isolation* the issue of terrorism can be read as the extreme form of the patriarchal nihilism identified in texts such as *August is a Wicked Month* and *Casualties of Peace*, while O'Brien's engagement with abortion law in *Down by the River* is the culmination of her ambiguous representations of maternity. Mary's incestuous and underage pregnancy is paralleled by her mother's simultaneously developing cancer. This can be read as an extension of episodes such as Kate's voluntary sterilization and the 'immobilizing' mother–daughter relationships of *A Pagan Place* and *Night*.[6]

Throughout the trilogy, the convergence of 'issues' and deconstructions of masculinity allows for the exploration of alternative possibilities. Each of the novels ends on a note of qualified optimism. *House of Splendid Isolation* is framed by the voice of Josie's long since aborted child, who refers to 'the knowledge that is yet to be'. In the retrospective context of *Mother Ireland* this suggests a state of arrested potential in which 'masculine' and 'feminine' can meet. *Down by the River* finishes with its protagonist's triumphal song, while at the end of *Wild Decembers* Breege is seen as a 'warrior queen' 'holding it together' as she anticipates the birth of her child. It is no accident that Sophia Hillan King's essay on the trilogy, is entitled 'On the Side of Life'; throughout the trilogy O'Brien presents the maternal imaginary exemplified by Catalina as a lifegiving alternative to 'nihilism'.

But 'nihilism' is unsparingly represented. *House of Splendid Isolation*'s analysis of the actions and motives of republican and Garda alike exposes the commonality of patriarchal domination within Ireland, illustrating the extent to which:

> In male culture, police are heroic and so are outlaws; males who enforce standards are heroic and so are those who violate them. The conflicts between these groups embody the male commitment to violence . . .[7]

In the context of the Irish woman/writer's access to language and the symbolic order, it is significant that each novel in the trilogy recounts instances of women 'silenced' by men. In *House of Splendid Isolation* the fugitive McGreevy encounters a policeman's young daughter. Telling her that 'he [is] starving, he'd eat a young child', he makes her feel 'as if she had no tongue at all'. Tellingly, the girl's response to her father is similar: 'I have no tongue'. The male capacity to silence is universalized (*HSI* 100–101). Later Josie tells McGreevy: 'You've silenced us all' (*HSI* 111). She herself has been silenced by her late husband James, 'allowing no whimper of pain or even protest to escape her lips' as he beats her (*HSI* 135). Josie is ultimately shot by the Garda; because she is wearing a man's coat they mistake her for McGreevy. She is 'struck speechless' as she dies (*HSI* 205).

In *Down by the River* the young protagonist is wholly unable to articulate her plight. Visiting a shrine, she leaves a coded message for a god who does not speak her language: 'Please cure my father's epilepsy' (*DR* 68). It is intertextually significant that the chapter in which James Macnamara forces his daughter into oral sex is headed 'A Pagan Place', recalling not only the *Pagan Place* narrator's subjection to priest and father, but the way in which she is forced to 'sing dumb'. After the event:

> Nothing would drag a word out of [Mary], not threats, not coaxing . . . Her tongue was gone. It lay there like the tongue of an old shoe. It was stiff and defiled. Her tongue had become an enemy. (*DR* 29)

Later a policeman explains Mary's silence: 'Shame, I've seen it before . . . Often . . . they feel dirtier if they tell it . . . They feel they're to blame in some way' (*DR* 227).[8]

In *Wild Decembers* the protagonist Breege is also silenced by pregnancy. Her one sexual encounter with her lover Bugler takes place on an island featuring a round tower and tombstones, again recalling *A Pagan Place*. Their lovemaking is described as 'that nascent nearness in which self is lost'. The echo of the 'wandering milky watery bliss' experienced by Anna and Catalina is significant since transcendence of the dominant discourse is only temporary. Furthermore, lovemaking takes place within a landscape defined by the masculine. Afterwards Breege is unable to recover her self. When she discovers that she is pregnant she goes to church and climbs into the nativity set. The sacristan discovers 'Breege Brennan lying in the straw alongside the donkey, the zebra, the infant Jesus and the Holy Family' in a tragic parody of the Irish Catholic maternal ideal (*WD* 191). Breege 'tries [to explain] but the words won't come'; she is subsequently taken to an asylum (*WD* 192). It is significant that Breege and, in *Down by the River*, Mary, recover their 'voices' only within the dominant discourse. Breege sings the 'song Bugler had given her' (*WD* 204) while Mary shines at a karaoke session on a winter evening redolent of Joyce's 'The Dead': 'Across the land the snow is falling . . .' (*DR* 264).

Intertextuality is further deployed towards analysis of patriarchal accounts of 'femininity'. In *House of Splendid Isolation* constructions of Josie are historically grounded. O'Brien's account of the relationship between Josie and McGreevy shows how:

> [The terrorist] mystique is the latest version of the Demon Lover [who] emanates sexual power because he represents obliteration. He excites with the mind of fear. He is the essential challenge to tenderness . . . whether [women] collaborate or beg, support or approve, always it is a case of *cherchez l'homme*.[9]

There is tension, though, between this position and historical evidence of women's desire for active involvement in nationalism. Constance Markievicz, for example, exhorted the Irish Women's Franchise League to:

> dress suitably in short skirts and strong boots, leave your jewels . . . and buy a revolver. Don't trust to your 'feminine charm' and your capacity for getting on the soft side of men but take up your responsibilities and be prepared to go your own way . . .[10]

Addressing these contradictions, Gerardine Meaney points out that:

> Women have been actively involved in every possible variant of
> nationalism and unionism . . . Women have supported and carried
> out violent actions . . . If patriarchal history has portrayed us as
> bystanders to the political process, it has lied. We have always
> been implicated, even in our own oppression.[11]

Josie's oppression by 'patriarchal history' is underscored by
her appearance as Anglo-American Lady of Shalott, sighing
'Oh those darned shadows' as 'things g[e]t darker, gloomier,
more oppressive' within her marriage (*HSI* 32). Like the Lady
of Shalott, Josie is an icon trapped in her own home, firstly by
her marriage to James and later by McGreevy. To her adoring
servant Paud – who having directed McGreevy to her house is
indirectly responsible for her death – she is 'Queen of the
Munster Fairies' (*HSI* 62). McGreevy himself reflects on her
'wild, staring, Virgin Mary eyes' (*HSI* 63). Josie does attempt
briefly to free herself from 'Mother Ireland' constructions by
making nationalism her own; escaping from McGreevy she
'hums loudly, a Fenian song, the only one she knows, about a
woman gathering nettles [for food]'.[12] But the song goes:
'Glorio . . . Glorio to the bold Fenian *men*' (my emphasis) and
'very soon she is winded' (*HSI* 80). Josie's entrapment in
'femininity' is signified by her alignment with the 'Colleen
Bawn', a jilted ballad heroine 'who was drowned and whose
death was traced later by the appearance of a corset on the
water' (*HSI* 35–6). Josie is beaten by James after Paud discovers
her own corset by the lake, where she has removed it in
anticipation of an encounter with Father John the priest (*HSI*
132–3).

Throughout the trilogy the protagonists' names are intertextually significant. McGreevy's reference to Josie's 'Virgin Mary'
eyes pre-empts not only Mary Macnamara, but Breege in *Wild
December* whose local nickname is 'Ivory Mary'. This suggests
the servitude of all three women to the Irish maternal ideal,
which is invalidated when the pregnant Mary Macnamara
visits a shrine in desperation. The 'painted Virgin' in the shrine
is significantly 'held up' by 'pillows of blue vapour' (*WD* 68).
Furthermore, Mary is ashamed to look at the statue in her own
home, feeling that 'Maybe Our Lady knew' (*WD* 7). After her
'fall' she is reinvented as 'Magdalen', the code name given to
her when her attempt to seek abortion in England becomes the

81

topic for a radio phone-in. The gap between 'Magdalen' and cultural ideal is exemplified by a politician's reference to 'some little slut about to pour piss on the nation's breast'; here a feminized 'Mother Ireland' is invoked in condemnation of 'her' errant daughter (*WD* 340). References to Irish literary monoliths compound Mary's disempowerment; the guard PJ is challenged by his mistress Geraldine: 'Hundreds of girls go [to England for abortions] . . . Including me . . . Why one law for us and one for some poor girl' (*WD* 159). After their resultant row, Geraldine anticipates that PJ will send her 'a poem, Yeats, who else'.[13] The wife of a diplomat involved in Mary's case is 'a Joycean scholar'; this suggests that women can advance only through engagement with the dominant discourse (*WD* 162).

Sophia Hillan King notes that the name of Breege in *Wild Decembers* 'recalls St Brigid, Ireland's own Mary'. Identifying implicit intertextualities in this novel, Hillan King argues that 'a strong element of magic realism pervades the narrative, as if this were a story by the brothers Grimm that is being played out in everyday life'. 'The Crock', a deformed and menacing local who betrays Breege to her brother Joseph and thereby triggers Bugler's death, is identified as 'Caliban-like [in his] revenge upon the beautiful and good girl he covets for himself'. Hillan King's essay offers a vital counterpart to Clare Boylan's argument that *Wild Decembers* 'would have been more chilling and true' had it been 'set against a contemporary backdrop' rather than in the 1970s.[14] Hillan King reveals the instrumentality of O'Brien's 'magic realism' to the exposition of ongoing cultural 'truths'. Identifying Joycean references such as echoes of 'The Dead' in Breege's song, she argues that O'Brien 'echoes the verbal dexterity and deadly wit of Joyce', demonstrating that she is 'proud to be Irish'.[15] Without disputing O'Brien's admiration for and indebtedness to Joyce, I would argue that her deployment of intertextuality reinforces Breege's social and cultural oppression. The closure of *Wild Decembers* hints at the need for alternative intertextualities and recovery of the matriarchal culture of the warrior queens.

Wild Decembers' concluding image of Breege can be read as an antidote to the distortions of maternity which resonate throughout the trilogy, signifying cultural ambivalence towards motherhood and the maternal body. I have already suggested that the narrative voice which frames *House of Splendid Isolation* – that of Josie's aborted child – indicates pre-natal potential and arrested development. O'Brien deploys similarly ambivalent imagery in her introduction of McGreevy. He is first seen hiding 'inside the hollow of a tree once struck by lightning', a position which is analogized with 'cradle and coffin, foetus and corpse'. By linking birth and death, this imagery reinforces McGreevy's nihilism. Indeed, the deathly image of 'foetus and corpse' suggests that the terrorist son of 'Mother Ireland' is rotten in the womb and that constructions of Ireland as 'devouring' need to be revised. Ironically McGreevy is later seen in a travesty of the Nativity, hiding in 'a manger of straw' (*HSI* 13). This recalls the image of McGreevy as nihilistic 'foetus' and anticipates Breege's retreat to the manger, which contributes retrospectively to McGreevy's feminization. The alignment of McGreevy with Christ is reinforced by Rory's revelation that he and his fellow Guards – who are seeking out McGreevy – are known as 'the three wise men' (*HSI* 9). McGreevy is further feminized by his capacity for tenderness. When his sojourn in the manger is interrupted by a cow going into labour, he delivers the calf and is moved by 'the impossible licking love of it' (*HSI* 15). This is poignantly contrasted with the nihilism inherent in human relationships; McGreevy recalls how when he was taken to view his dead child – the victim along with her mother of a revenge killing – the police 'searched the white habit for explosives' (*HSI* 13).

The sterility suggested by the image of infant corpse as agent of destruction is compounded by accounts of Josie's marriage and abortion. 'Femininity' and 'maternity' are conflated in and signified by references to Josie's corset, which identifies her as 'Colleen Bawn' and impairs her fertility. The maidservant Brid speculates: 'The Missus didn't want a baby ... Wore corsets that were too tight' (*HSI* 45). An accoutrement of 'femininity' is deployed towards denying James paternity. James himself compares Josie with: 'Wet fields, brown clay through the blades of grass, fields like graveyards, undug' (*HSI* 43). In the wake of the foetus/corpse analogy, this can be read in the context of nationalism, which affects not only 'mother country' but Josie as potential mother. As Gerardine Meaney points out:

The images of suffering *Mother Ireland* and the self-sacrificing mother are difficult to separate. Both serve to obliterate the reality of women's lives. Both seek to perpetuate an image of Woman far from the experience, expectations and ideals of contemporary women.[16]

When Josie does become pregnant she feels unsurprisingly that 'it was not a normal child': 'It cried inside the walls of her womb. It was more like a banshee than a child' (*HSI* 46). The foetus/corpse analogy is further reinforced; banshees traditionally herald death. Josie records in her diary:

I was not ready for a child. The crib that [James] brought up from the cellar was the most forlorn looking thing. It had belonged to his people. It felt alien. I couldn't see myself rocking it. (*HSI* 195)

Josie struggles against matrilineage as well as patrilineage, becoming convinced that 'This child and her mother were one, in league against her' (*HSI* 48). Within the context of *House of Splendid Isolation*, maternal failure is historicized. James perceives Josie as 'devouring', while his friend constructs her as '*Sheela-na-gig*' – a reference to carvings found in Irish churches which feature women holding open their vaginas (*HSI* 109). This echoes *Mother Ireland*'s citation of Joyce's analogy of Ireland with a 'sow' devouring her 'young' and aligns her with the 'Ireland' for 'whom' McGreevy is prepared to kill (*MI* 11).

As her maternal instincts are culturally thwarted, Josie finds a child substitute in the bizarre sculpture given to her by Father John; her response to the gift 'gr[ows] bigger and sturdier . . . like a child swelling up in her' (*HSI* 131). Sensing this, James quips that they should 'christen it, give it a name' (*HSI* 130). Yet Josie is left associating their unconsummated affair with:

ugly things, lumpen, brutish . . . like a big goose egg being skewered with a knitting needle, the juices leaking and dripping out of her . . . (*HSI* 134)

This anticipates the 'skewer[ing]' to which Josie is subjected during her abortion, when she is given – grotesquely:

a thing to hold. It was a mesh basket with a false eggshell inside and when pressed the shell parted and a chicken popped up and squeaked, a yellow cloth chicken. I tried to imagine that the wire was skewering its gullet instead of me. (*HSI* 195)

The 'false' eggshell signifies the mendacity of a culture of maternity centred around a virgin birth. Cultural matricide drives Josie to infanticide, and as she ages she endures 'the vacant, shriven years of it' by becoming a substitute mother to James.[17] Only before her death, and in response to McGreevy's desire 'to have children, wains' once 'the country [is] one', does she experience the maternal instinct which in the contexts of a divided 'Mother Ireland' and Josie's age is dismissed as a 'lunatic ... longing' (*HSI* 189).

Down by the River continues to address the issue of abortion within Ireland, where, as Meaney argues, mythology and law intersect. Meaney reveals that:

> The assumption that the law needed to intervene in the relationship between woman and foetus – to protect the so-called 'unborn child' from its mother – is indicative of a deep distrust and fear of women. This distrust and fear is paradoxically rooted in the idealization of the mother in Irish culture as an all-powerful, dehumanizing figure.[18]

In *Down by the River*, O'Brien reveals the extent to which women collude in such constructions; pro-lifers and liberals alike compete over Mary, who feels that they are 'all vying with each other as to who was in charge, who owned her' (*DR* 151). Yet this is done 'in the name of the father'; the anti-abortionist Roisin is sanctioned by secular and religious law. As Meaney points out:

> Such women seek to perpetuate the idealised virgin/mother figure of women so that they can *be* that figure. Such identification offers women one of the few roles of power available to them in patriarchy ... The attractions of the traditional feminine role ... are grounded in a deep distrust and loathing of femininity, however, and those women who identify with it are also expressing a form of self-hatred ... They are unable to accept themselves as thinking, choosing, sexual, intellectual ... and instead cling to a fantasy of women as simple handmaids of the lord.[19]

Meaney argues further that: 'Patriarchy's strongest hold over women is its ability to promote this inner division, which inhibits women's will for change ... and sets them campaigning against their own interests'. In *Down by the River*, Roisin – 'a beautiful girl with such lovely hair and such very special eyes' – initially appears as 'charming' but her fellow pro-lifers become 'terrified' of her (*DR* 17):

> It was when she began preaching that they became afraid, they saw something else, the eyes with the hardness of enamel, outrage in her voice, the insistence ... that they know how the brutal operation is done (*DR* 22).

Roisin's 'hardness' is a manifestation of her 'recruitment' by and collusion in social imperialism. Images of 'Our Lady ... her fingernails dirty from rooting in trash bins to find [aborted] foetuses and save them from dogs and human scavengers' help to reinforce cultural ideals of maternity. A contrasting image in the abortion clinic leaflet reflects the kind of woman who is assumed to reject maternity – 'a geisha, all tresses and come-hithers' (*DR* 131). O'Brien exposes the tensions between what men find attractive and what patriarchy is prepared to sanction.

Cultural ambivalence to 'maternity' is clearly exemplified by the immobilized relationship between Mary and her mother Bridget (whose name anticipates Breege in *Wild Decembers*). After Bridget's death Mary reflects that 'She had loved her mother too much and not enough' (*DR* 56). It is significant that Mary is raped and impregnated by James when wearing her mother's 'black dress'; mother and daughter are seen as 'feminized' and interchangeable commodities (*DR* 83). Bridget's arrested potential is revealed by the contrasting perceptions of James and Mary. While James reflects that: 'She could have been president of this country' Mary 'thinks of her mother combating their poverty with the eggs she sold' (*DR* 60). It is significant that Bridget is able to remain solvent only by selling the eggs to which she has an extreme aversion, perhaps because she perceives motherhood as a factor in her own commodification. The egg reference recalls Josie's abortion, while Bridget's death – a grotesque parody of giving birth – recalls the 'foetus/corpse' imagery surrounding McGreevy. In the retrospective light of *House of Splendid Isolation*, it is significant that Bridget's cancer is politicized within an Irish context. As Bridget looks around a mushroom farm and compares the spores to those 'inside her' she learns about 'the losses incurred from blight and hearing that word she s[ees] the black and rotting cavities of blighted potatoes' (*DR* 45–6). Like Mary, Bridget is aligned with the diseased maternal body of 'Mother Ireland', 'raped' by 'her' colonizers. Irishness, suffering and maternity are most specifically linked by a doctor who remarks: 'Rosaries and ovaries, I don't know which does the most damage to this country' (*DR* 116). It is, of course, perceptions of 'rosaries and ovaries' which do the damage; the cultural ideal of maternity is threatened by the bodily functions which it struggles to deny. Cultural matricide is highlighted by the alignment of Bridget's cancer with Mary's pregnancy, itself an unwanted and destructive growth.

In the context of cultural matricide, it is significant that the rural society of *Wild Decembers* is broadly depicted as sterile. At the opening of the novel, the protagonist's brother Joseph informs their neighbour: 'You won't find a child around here' (*WD* 6), while at the village tea 'no one wants to be mother'. Joseph and Breege, orphaned brother and sister, live together in a relationship which offers no scope for fertility or inheritance.[20] Immobilization and distortion are linked again with a diseased and sterile 'Mother Ireland'; the potato famine is recorded as having hit Cloontha 'on Our Lady's Eve'. Images of 'devouring' and 'castrated' mothers recur throughout the text; at the chapel O'Brien shows:

> Two different reactions to the same call from a young baby in need. Two women, mothers. One exemplifying worldly selfishness and the other willing to sacrifice herself for her young. (*WD* 199)

Given her immobilization between these equally undesirable alternatives, it is not surprising that Breege's response to her pregnancy is to lose her power of speech (*WD* 188–9). But *Wild Decembers* does seem to offer a third path. Sophia Hillan King affirms that:

> O'Brien presents us at the end, not with an answer, but with a passionate expression of hope that Breege and her child and all who have gone before them may transcend all that would snare them . . .[21]

This offers in turn the possibility of transcending social and symbolic orders which collude in cultural matricide. The novel's concluding image of Breege 'holding her belly' suggests once more the pre-natal potential explored in *Mother Ireland* and *The High Raod*.

The need to revise social and symbolic orders is suggested by the trilogy's attention to 'masculinity' as well as to 'femininity' and 'maternity'. The trilogy's most overt suggestion that these are 'performative acts' is *Down by the River*'s representation of Reginald, a 'drag' performer with whom Mary and her friend Betty stay when they first attempt to procure an abortion for Mary in England. Recalling the transvestite stripper in *August is a Wicked Month* Reginald shows Mary and Betty 'his several costumes, his spangly things and his leather' and performs 'a song which Billie Holiday, his heroine, used to sing'. As in *August is a Wicked Month*, Reginald's grotesque parody of 'femininity' serves to expose the 'performative acts' of his audience. In *Down by the River*, though, the drag act highlights the tyranny of biological destiny. Even in drag Reginald is clearly defined as male:

> He left the room and returned in a beaded dress that was sleeveless and skimpy ... His legs and knees looked buckled and underfed but he gained confidence as soon as he stepped on the pouffe ... Up there he pouted and curled his finger at one or the other and said 'I think I'll have you ...' (*DR* 140–41)

Despite the pathetic camp of Reginald's 'act' he has the 'confidence' of the male who is permitted a choice of gender roles.

Down by the River offers less overt analysis of men 'play[ing]' with 'masculinity'. The limitations of the roles on offer are suggested – as in *House of Splendid Isolation* – by O'Brien's representations of police and republicans alike. In *House of Splendid Isolation* police violence is exemplified by Rory's passion for deer-hunting; despite his romantic response to 'purple mountains' and trees, he is able to commune with nature only by killing (*HSI* 10). Furthermore, the shooting of deer is implicitly compared to the shooting of 'young men coming down from the North', who, in turn incite fear 'with their guns and their hoods' (*HSI* 9). After shooting the deer, though, Rory and his fellows 'wash[ing] their hands in the stream are like penitents ... seeking intercession for something fateful that is to be' (*HSI* 199–201). This suggests discomfort with 'masculine' 'conflict' and 'violence'. The anticipation of 'the knowledge that is to be' identified by Josie's child acknowledges the need for new social and symbolic orders for men as well as women. It has been argued that men:

> have learnt to pride [them]selves in [their] struggles against [their] own desires and natures, to be able to identify [their] sense of self with [their] reason. If successful, this denial can mean that [they] no longer have a sense of self which exists separately from [their] sense of male identity.[22]

Thus McGreevy is ably to deny the 'self' that longs for peace and 'wains', just as Rory is able to subsume his affinity with nature to destruction.

House of Splendid Isolation's intertextualities question 'masculinity' along with 'femininity'. Again, names are intertextually significant – 'James' recalls the violent father of the earlier trilogy whilst anticipating James Macnamara. McGreevy is specifically analogized with heroes of Ireland's past such as Cuchullain. Male responses to these constructions are by no means straightforward; the Southern Irish Garda are supposedly on the side of law rather than nationalism, and McGreevy as a Northern nationalist feels excluded by 'the sunny South where people had time for love and strawberries [and] forgot their brothers and sisters across the border' (*HSI* 57). But collusion between men is exemplified in the 'Last Days' section of the novel when the guards observing the 'big house' plot McGreevy's arrest while simultaneously paying homage to his perceived heroism. Ned, for example, recites a poem about Michael Collins, remarking: 'There'll be a poem about this soon' (*HSI* 177). Here O'Brien reinforces the co-dependence of 'myth' and 'masculinity'. The Garda's tendency to lionize McGreevy is further emphasized by Cormac likening him to Cuchullain (*HSI* 188). Yet McGreevy himself has denied this construction from the very outset of the novel, pointing out to his accomplice: 'I'm not fucking Cuchullain' (*HSI* 18). McGreevy's dilemma is further underscored by his feminization throughout the text. As a Northerner he is as 'interred in the mesh of fable' as his Southern counterparts, yet his identity is complicated by exile (*HSI* 57). It is significant that Josie records McGreevy's history and grievances in her diary, weaving another 'fairytale' for them both:

'The South forgot us,' he said. Forlorn. Aggrieved. A likeness to those children in fable banished, exiled in lakes for hundreds of years, cut off from the homeland. (HSI 99)

The Northern republican male is seen – like the Southern female narrator of *Mother Ireland* – as 'exiled' and 'longing to return to the lost home (womb) of the mother'.[23] This 'longing' is manifested through terrorism. The conclusion to *House of Splendid Isolation* again conflates exile from womb and mother country, arguing that 'the knowledge that is to be' is that it is necessary 'to go right into the heart of the hate and the wrong and to sup from it and be supped' (*HSI* 216). The 'body' analogy suggests that the 'hate and wrong' which needs to be resolved exists not only between political factions but also between men and women.

The need for resolution between the sexes further informs *Down by the River*. As I have already argued, James Macnamara is represented throughout the text not as a monster, but as a victim of social and symbolic orders along with his daughter. The 14-year-old girl on whom Mary Macnamara is based was raped by a family friend; by transposing 'friend' to 'father', O'Brien moves the threat of violence even closer to home, reinforcing the point that: 'Interacting with other patriarchal social structures, rape functions as a mechanism of social control to keep women in their place' and that ultimately: 'Through rape myths, the state and male ideologies legitimate and conceal male violence against women'.[24] But James functions not only as a cog in the social mechanism, but – in the light of Irigaray's commentary on incest – as something of a spanner in the works.[25] Leonard points out that under Southern Irish law: 'If forced incest takes place between father and daughter, it is classified as incest rather than rape' – with a lighter sentence.[26] This sanctions 'daughter' as 'property', since rape is legally classified as such only when perpetrated by a male other than the father. Legalities aside, in breaking the incest taboo James violates the laws of exchange between men.[27] In this context James's disruption of social and symbolic orders is significant. While not suggesting for a moment that O'Brien sanctions incest or rape, she does position James as victim. From an Irigarayan perspective his blood – the crucial

90

factor in patrilineage – is 'destabilized' by being 'dispatched to Oxford to undergo a test' for the court hearing (*HSI* 249).

The male subject's accession to 'masculinity' is examined not only through James but through lawyers and politicians. When PJ is called by the Attorney General:

> Suddenly he is not Jock, or rather he is the other Jock, the one Geraldine [his mistress] recoils from . . . The smiling blushing gallant put to one side now like a photograph overlaid with another; cold, pugnacious, asking without words why in feck's name she has come out of the bathroom . . . (*HSI* 158).

The judge in Mary's case revels in his own 'mastery', recalling his boyhood self-perceptions: 'Sometimes . . . he got up and went out into the garden and in the moonlight hit a few balls with a hurl-stick and re-imagined himself in the fields, the stony fields of long ago, his mind like the leather ball itself, an acceleration to it' (*DR* 241). 'Masculinity' is seen throughout *Down by the River* as compulsory; as Hillan King points out, the only overtly feminized male in the text is 'punished for it' – Luke is 'the gentle hippy boy who shelters [Mary]'.[28] Luke 'suffers through association' with Mary; his 'type' are dismissed by Guard Fahy as 'lice on the locks of the nation' (*DR* 172). The 'feminized' sons of 'Mother Ireland' are perceived as parasitic. While, as Hillan King points out, James – like his namesake in *House of Splendid Isolation* – is 'feminized' by his tenderness to his horse, society operates, as the judges point out, like 'horse-trading' (*DR* 253). Women and horses are commodities and as such are not to be identified with. The ambiguous ending of *Down by the River* reiterates the need for social and symbolic orders to be revised. Mary triumphs only over 'feminized' 'masculinity'.

Wild Decembers continues O'Brien's analysis of the extent to which collusion in 'masculinity' results only in social deadlock. Land ownership is posited as the privilege of the 'warring sons of warring sons' of Ireland, but the battle between Joseph and Bugler results only in the death of one and imprisonment of the other (*WD* 2). Bugler is significantly nicknamed 'the Shepherd' 'because of having worked on a sheep station' in Australia (*WD* 4). Like McGreevy he is 'feminized' by his exile; constructed as 'wild colonial boy' and womanizer he is nonetheless capable of moments of extreme tenderness towards Breege and his Australian fiancée Rosemary (*WD* 25). Joseph's solicitor identifies the social 'inferiority of the returned exile' who endures not only 'slights, insults, other races calling him a Paddy or a Mick' but 'displacement ... the longing for home' (*WD* 91). Joseph fares little better; like his sister Breege he is immobilized by biblical construction, as 'Joseph of Arimathea' (*WD* 10). Joseph's affinity with the landscape and recognition that, 'God was not a bearded man in the sky but here ... In Cloontha ... alone with nature' points to his desire to avoid stereotype, but he experiences his body as a 'crippled virginal baulk' (*WD* 19, 137). The comparison of Joseph to a culturally immobilized Christ anticipates his appearance as 'a crucified shape of pity' after shooting Bugler (*WD* 230). Like McGreevy and James Macnamara before him, he is 'feminized' through disempowerment by the colonizer, in this case the Anglo-Irish Lady Harkness who deprives Breege of her 'kingdoms' by leasing land to Bugler rather than to Joseph (*WD* 61). O'Brien's representation of the colonizer as female further complicates the issues surrounding 'masculinity' and 'femininity' which she has addressed throughout the trilogy. *Wild December*'s triumphal closing image of Breege 'holding it together' is in turn qualified by Breege's 'hope that there is communion between living and dead, between those, who even in their most stranded selves are on the side of life and harbingers of love' (*WD* 244). Within the existing social and symbolic orders Breege and Bugler, like Cathy and Heathcliff before them, can 'commune' only from opposite 'sides'. But O'Brien's tribute to her 'literary mother' does suggest the potential for revisions of these orders, particularly in the light of her ongoing deconstructions of 'Mother Ireland'. Cultural geographer Catherine Nash argues that:

> rather than simply assert the oppressive nature of images of feminised landscapes or women's bodies as terrain, it is necessary to engage with them, to disrupt their authority and open up possibilities for difference, subversion, resistance and reappropriation.[29]

This is a strategy which O'Brien seems increasingly to deploy.

8

'The Other Half of Ireland':
James Joyce

In 1984 Edna O'Brien revealed:

> at one point I thought of writing a book on Joyce, *comme tout le monde*! I read lots of books about Joyce and wrote a monograph. Then I realized that there were already too many books on him and that the best thing you could read about Joyce was Joyce himself.[1]

In 1999 O'Brien's biography of Joyce was published by Weidenfeld and Nicolson for their *Lives* series, the concept of which was to invite contemporary writers to comment on literary and cultural icons such as Joyce, Proust and Mozart. In this chapter I shall argue that by 1999 O'Brien was ready to address issues which have already been examined in relation to her fiction and autobiography; namely the woman writer's struggle for self-realization in the shadow of the literary father; cultural constructions of 'femininity' and maternity, including that of 'Mother Ireland'; 'masculinity'; gender and language.

The interviews and reviews which followed the publication of *James Joyce* do not necessarily acknowledge the text as the logical outcome or culmination of O'Brien's engagement with these issues, but they reveal much about ongoing perceptions of O'Brien in relation to Joyce. Anne Haverty echoes O'Brien's early reservations about writing on Joyce, claiming that O'Brien's contribution 'could not be called a herculean achievement ... since Joyce is among the most written-about writers in history'. But Haverty unwittingly identifies the uniqueness of O'Brien's *James Joyce*, observing that: 'Seeking his essence, she assumes his own messianic view of himself'.[2] This suggests the problematic nature of O'Brien's engagement with her literary father, which O'Brien herself addresses in an interview with Brian Case. Acknowledging: 'I have not learned as much from anyone as I have from Joyce over the years', O'Brien recounts buying T. S. Eliot's *Introducing James Joyce* and 'open[ing] it at random at the Christmas dinner in *Portrait of the Artist'*. It is not difficult to identify the genesis of the 'Christmas' episode in *Mother Ireland* in which the family life of 'Edna' is seen as predetermined by Joyce: 'long before – but you did not know it'. (*MI* 74). Commenting on her biography, O'Brien affirms: 'I have served him. This is my hymn to him'. The Case interview reveals much about the root of O'Brien's desire to 'serve'. Crucially, O'Brien identifies Joyce as 'hav[ing] the sensibility of a man and a woman'. In the light of the nineties trilogy's attention to 'masculinity' it is significant that O'Brien devotes much of *James Joyce* to analysis of language and gender, particularly through her account of Joyce's relationship with Nora Barnacle.

Predictably, though, this was trivialized by some reviewers. John O'Mahoney remarks somewhat dismissively that '[O'Brien] is best when dealing with the women in Joyce's life', making no attempt to analyse why this might be. Instead he resorts to cheap humour, likening *James Joyce* to 'a biography of Ivan the Terrible by Jilly Cooper'.[3] O'Mahoney misses the point that O'Brien identifies Joyce himself as 'a romantic when it came to women', offering some astute analysis of Joyce's attitudes to women within their social and cultural contexts (*JJ* 84).

O'Brien is eminently qualified to comment on these contexts, and her identification with Joyce is revealed not only by responses to *James Joyce*, but by the text itself. In the Case interview O'Brien implicitly likens Joyce's need 'to experience everything' with her own experiments with 'LSD with RD Laing'. Further commonalities are revealed: 'When I was growing up in Ireland, words and language became my friend and weapon against all the rest of the world'. In the light of Toril Moi's observation on the intersection of fiction and autobiography – to which might be added 'biography' – it is significant that *James Joyce* opens 'Once upon a time . . .' (*JJ* 1).

Conflating the 'stories' of Joyce and his own Stephen Dedalus, this opening also embraces the 'story' of Joyce's literary daughter. O'Brien's references to Joyce's family echo and parallel her autobiographical and fictional commentaries; she recounts, for example, the extent to which Joyce 'was haunted by [his mother's] memory' and argues that '*Ulysses* ... would have killed her had she not already died' (*JJ* 17–18). In her interview with Shusha Guppy O'Brien reflects – with particular reference to Ireland – that: 'Even when the parents die, you dream of them as if they were still there', and reveals the 'sadness', 'anger' and 'pity' which she experienced on her mother's rejection of *The Country Girls*.[4] Commenting in *James Joyce* on the response of writers' families to their representation in literature O'Brien argues that: 'The writer exposes and reinforces their shame in themselves and they cannot forgive it' (*JJ* 19). Later she refers to 'writers and their mothers' as 'the uncharted deep', an image which again suggests the 'unstable' female fluids examined in *The High Road* (*JJ* 22).

But O'Brien's identification with Joyce does not eradicate the problematic nature of his role as literary father. Admitting that 'Anyone who touched Joyce seemed to get a bit carried away', O'Brien affirms: 'His shade haunts every great writer who has followed him' (*JJ* 99, 171). It is crucial that O'Brien raises the question of 'who owns Joyce' since her contribution is 'about' not ownership, but relationship. Commenting on Joyce's relationship with his brother Stanislaus, O'Brien writes that 'James had become surrogate father and living persecutor' (*JJ* 53). In the context of Joyce's role as O'Brien's literary father it is significant that 'James' has been a recurrent name for the 'living persecutors' of her fiction, from James Brady in *The Country Girls* to James Macnamara in *Down by the River*. Throughout the biography, O'Brien herself deploys Joycean discourse; as reviewers noted, it is not always easy to distinguish between unacknowledged quotation and pastiche. To dismiss this as poor scholarship is simplistic; like *A Pagan Place* and *Night, James Joyce* reveals the extent to which O'Brien is both indebted to and constrained by her literary father, particularly in its use of intertextuality. Her account of Nora Barnacle's 'near seduction by a young curate' recalls the *Pagan Place* narrator's encounter with the priest, and a description of her as "the bride" in a man's long overcoat' echoes Josie at the climactic point of *House of Splendid Isolation* (*JJ* 44–5).

It is significant that O'Brien's biography of Joyce is largely 'about' Nora Barnacle; *James Joyce's* intertextualities conflate 'Nora' not only with O'Brien's fictional characters, but implicitly with O'Brien herself. O'Brien recounts how Nora 'copied [a] letter [to Joyce] from a book of etiquette'; this recalls Caithleen's intention to copy out a letter to Eugene from *Wuthering Heights* (*JJ* 40). On a more sinister note – and moving on from the Joyces' courtship to their marriage – O'Brien reveals that:

> while she penned her grievances, Joyce suggested icily that she should try using the capital letter for the word 'I'. He was not so intolerant of this lapse when he sat down to write Molly Bloom's galloping soliloquy. (*JJ* 52)

O'Brien's tart observation highlights the gap between appropriated and lived language and experience. This gap is similarly highlighted in O'Brien's account of Nora taking in washing to supplement the family income:

> Years later, in *Finnegan's Wake* two washerwomen would regale each other with the vices and wrongdoings of their customers. But Nora Barnacle had no washerwoman friend, no one to commune with, except her husband and then mostly in bed. (*JJ* 49)

Similarly O'Brien observes that: 'As a writer and dreamer [Joyce] could imagine that which he did not have, but for [Nora] there were no such poetic ascensions' (*JJ* 57–8). Lamenting: 'If only she had kept a diary', O'Brien attempts throughout *James Joyce* to reconstruct 'Nora' and to tell her story (*JJ* 57).

But O'Brien is not, as one critic would have it, out to represent Joyce 'as a cruel, scavenging egomaniac'.[5] Not only does O'Brien acknowledge: 'That he managed to write and that she got through each listless day with her son is a tribute to both of them', she examines the gender boundaries which assigned the Joyces to their respective roles (*JJ* 57).

Commenting on Nora's 'sexual prowess' and its undoubted influence on Joyce, O'Brien identifies this as 'radical' since 'sexuality and maternity [are] thought to be contrary' (*JJ* 74–5). O'Brien presents this contradiction as intrinsic to Joyce's responses to his own mother May; whilst identifying her in his youth 'with the Virgin Mary' he recognized her as being 'like so many Irish mothers, a "cracked vessel for childbearing" ' (*JJ* 2–3). O'Brien recounts how:

> He wrote a hymn to the two mothers, the earthly and the celestial one. As an altar boy, the ritual and liturgy of the Catholic Church engendered a kind of ecstasy in him and the Virgin Mary in her tower of ivory was the creature he adored. (*JJ* 6)

Yet in assuming 'masculinity' Joyce rejects both mothers, 'cho[osing] to believe that Jesus was more son of God than of Mary' and 'banish[ing]' May (*JJ* 13, 171). Contradictorily, though, Joyce said of himself as a writer: 'I do not want to be a literary Jesus Christ', a position which implicitly rejects the patrilineage of the literary canon (*JJ* 77). According to O'Brien Joyce's ambivalence towards and rejection of his mother resulted in his being 'haunted by her memory' so that her epistolary style resurfaces in Molly Bloom's soliloquy – a 'haunting', which prefigures the disruption of Mary Hooligan's soliloquy by her mother Lil (*JJ* 17, 19).

'Earthly' and 'celestial' aspects of 'femininity' are conflated in a letter to Nora in which Joyce:

> remind[s] her of the first night in Ringsend when her long tickly fingers frigged him slowly until he came, gazing at him with saint-like eyes . . . (*JJ* 72)

Less attractively, Nora is later depicted as an 'Irish Mary at home resenting housework' while Joyce courted a Jewish 'pagan Mary', a neighbour who 'reminded him of a girl he saw years before in Dublin wading out to sea – his future Nausicaa' (*JJ* 87).

The association of woman and sea is significant in the context of suppression of female discourse. O'Brien reflects that for Joyce 'women were like rivers that flowed in their own ineluctable way', echoing *The High Road*'s often gender-ambiguous metaphors of fluidity (*JJ* 37). O'Brien records that Joyce's first sexual arousal occurred on hearing a young nurse urinating (*JJ* 7). Later O'Brien revises Joyce's association of 'woman' with 'unstable fluid', determinedly grounding 'Anna Livia' – Joyce's personification of the River Liffey – in reality

97

and implicitly revealing the dual commodification of 'woman' and 'landscape':

His inspiration for the hair of Anna Livia was the beautiful red hair of Livia Schmitz . . . but it was also the River Dartry streaked red from the empty canisters thrown out from the nearby dye works. (*JJ* 146–7)

O'Brien's agenda is not to condemn Joyce for colluding in commodification, but rather to deconstruct the concepts of 'femininity' and 'maternity' by which he was influenced, and which he too questions. Having affirmed that 'women were like rivers' for Joyce, O'Brien argues that in *Finnegan's Wake* '*people* were not only people, they were as well rivers.' (*JJ* 128; my italics). Like the 1990s trilogy, *James Joyce* pays significant attention to 'masculinity'. The opening page echoes Mary Hooligan's list of 'males as national subjects':

a jejune Jesuit . . . a lecher, a Christian brother in luxuriousness, a Joyce of all trades, a bullock befriending bard, a peerless mummer, a priestified kinchite, a quill-frocked friar, a timoneer, a pool-beg flasher and a man with the gift of the Irish majacule script. (*JJ* 1)

Later O'Brien argues that Nora 'allow[ed] him to be all things, the child-man, the man-child, the peeping Tom, and the grand seducer' (*JJ* 74). Arguing against rigid definition, O'Brien simultaneously highlights the fragmentation of masculine identity and Joyce's ambiguous position as colonized male. O'Brien points out that:

Joyce may have disliked the strangling mentality of Catholic Ireland but it was matched by an equal distaste for English imperialism. (*JJ* 106)

Joyce's position is distinguished from that of Anglo-Irish Yeats:

Yeats believed that the spirit of the ancients was his birthright and the inner source of his poetry whereas Joyce's birthright was a plaster virgin in Fairview . . . (*JJ* 15)

In the context of O'Brien's revisions of Yeatsian metaphors and discourse, Joyce is significantly 'feminized' by his alignment with Mary Hooligan. Interestingly, O'Brien records that 'Virginia Woolf called [*Ulysses*] 'underbred'', empathizing with her

Irish literary father rather than with her English literary mother (*JJ* 125). Joyce's relative lack of status is seen as motivating his desire to 'map' Ireland, a desire initially engendered by the family's frequent moves during which the young Joyce 'drew a skeleton map of the city in his mind' (*JJ* 10):

> He determined to reinvent the city where he had been marginalized, laughed at and barred from literary circles. (*JJ* 15)

O'Brien draws out the irony inherent in Joyce's responses to 'Ireland'; whilst the Dublin 'landscape was the first enthralment to his young and highly-charged being' his exclusion from its literary circles meant that he could conceptualize 'mother Ireland' only as 'stepmother Eirrean' (*JJ* 170, 82). Only after his death would he 'be rewarded by having snatches of his *Ulysses* transcribed on small bronze plaques and bevelled into the pavements which Leopold Bloom and others had trodden' (*JJ* 61).

Joyce's position as colonized male is paralleled with that of his father John, whose 'family was his empire'. O'Brien argues astutely that: 'Domination of them reaffirmed his power as a man' (*JJ* 27). Given the 'feminization' of the colonized male, it is significant that O'Brien expresses this particular father–son relationship in gender-ambiguous terms, recording that: 'When John Joyce ... died ... James sank into a Lear-like state of lamentation.' (*JJ* 151). Lear is, of course, 'lamenting' his lost daughter. O'Brien goes on to argue that Joyce 'assumed a symbiotic closeness' with his father; 'symbiosis' is a term perhaps more usually associated with the mother–child relationship. Given O'Brien's identification of gender ambiguity in Joyce, it is not surprising that she contests Louis Gillet's view that 'Joyce was a god, a god espoused to men only':

> For [Gillet] Joyce's empathy was male, had nothing to do with trifling affairs of the heart or the senses, was a current going from man to man without passing through the intermediary of female entrails. Hard to tally that with lines such as – 'Touch me. Soft eyes. Soft soft soft hand ...' (*JJ* 166)

In the contexts of language and gender, it is interesting that O'Brien takes issue not only with Gillet, but with feminist critics of Joyce. O'Brien contests Marilyn French's view that 'Joyce had a contempt for women', arguing that 'in his thoughts just as in his works, everything about him was both complex and paradoxical' (*JJ* 89). Similarly she takes issue with Kate Millett's assertion that Joyce 'engaged in the naive participation in the cult of the primitive woman'. O'Brien's response is that: 'There is nothing naive in Joyce and if he depicted women as sexually primitive he was more prescient than anyone before or since' (*JJ* 92). Her comment that Joyce 'decided that only would-be thinkers or feminists would expect a woman to be a man's equal' is significant; clearly she sees reconfiguring of the symbolic order as outreaching the 'equality feminism' denounced by Irigaray (*JJ* 47).[6] Her observation that: 'The Irish [are] doomed to express themselves in a language not their own' again implicitly feminizes Joyce, aligning the colonized male with the woman exiled from the symbolic order (*JJ* 50). O'Brien seems to see this position as the genesis of Joyce's experiments with language, arguing that: 'Language is the hero and heroine' of his works (*JJ* 97). In the light of Irigaray's suggestions for a symbolic order constructed around woman's genital lips rather than around the phallus, it is telling that O'Brien chooses to quote from *Finnegan's Wake* the line: 'twolips have pressed togatherthem' (*JJ* 147).[7]

Joyce's attempts to reconfigure the symbolic order in his fiction are paralleled with his 'real life' quest to realize 'the mystic's longing for a couple to dissolve into one' (*JJ* 74). O'Brien claims that 'Joyce wanted to wallow in the inner maelstrom of woman's desire' and refers to his 'talk[ing] and talk[ing] with "the little mother" [Nora] who would take him into the dark sanctuary of her womb' (*JJ* 73). O'Brien perceives Joyce as wishing to recover the state of pre-natal potential which she herself identifies at the end of *Mother Ireland*. Significantly, 'little mother' Nora and 'Mother Ireland' are conflated by O'Brien, who argues that:

> In her [Joyce] was to seek and find earth mother, dark, formless, made beautiful by moonlight. He was a Dubliner, she was from Galway; she was to bring in her jingles, her stories, her pisreogs the echoes of her ancestry, the other half of Ireland – soil, gloom, moon grey nettles, the warring clans and the mutinous Shannon waters. (*JJ* 37)

Given the association of Nora with the river Shannon, it is significant that O'Brien aligns Joyce's desire for recovery with his reconfiguration of language. O'Brien argues that:

> Joyce pored over words and dialect in order to create the new language or rather the old one, the one he believed existed in its pristine purity before tongues were jumbled.   (*JJ* 167)

O'Brien connects Joyce's feminization of language with the death of his mother which 'he had described "as a wound on the brain"' (*JJ* 170). Arguing that for him 'mother, words and sea [were] inseparable', she points out that 'he spoke of words as being the sea 'crashing in on his breaking brain'. O'Brien points out further that this conflation surfaces in his fiction: 'Bloom would muse on the womb-like state – "before born babe had bliss and won worship"' (*JJ* 170).

Throughout this biography Joyce's literary daughter achieves a fine balance between recognition of Joyce as 'living persecutor' and empathy with his position as colonized male. Her own act of resistance to this is to affirm that 'Joyce's finest epitaph came from Nora' (*JJ* 173). This demonstrates solidarity with Joyce in the face of a literary establishment which so often excluded him, but it also reaffirms the importance of 'the world of Nora Barnacle', reconstructing the woman who could not keep a diary.

It is impossible to draw any definitive conclusion from the work of a living and – in O'Brien's case – prolific writer, and it would be risky to speculate about the direction of her future work. The outlook seems optimistic, though. My opening chapter was partly a protest against critical dismissal of O'Brien as 'lightweight', but I must thankfully acknowledge that there have been recent signs of reassessment. Although the *Irish Times* review described the *James Joyce* project as 'the encounter of one distinguished sensibility and consciousness with those of an even more distinguished other' – and there are no prizes for guessing which was perceived as which – when Sophia Hillan King offered her citation for Edna O'Brien's honorary doctorate from the Queen's University of Belfast on 6 July 1999, she established O'Brien as 'this most accomplished *successor* to Joyce' (my italics). I can think of no more fitting note upon which to conclude this study.

9

In the Forest: A Country Boy

This study was intended to end with chapter 8, and with some heavily qualified closure outlining the problematics of drawing 'conclusions' about the work of a living and prolific writer. Sure enough, *In the Forest* [1] was published on 4 April 2002, just as Joanna Jellinek had copy-edited my supposedly completed script. Frustrating though this was, I am thankful to be able to add this chapter as I fully support David Godwin's promotion of the novel as 'possess[ing] the greatest delicacy and integrity'.[2]

Godwin's view is not without its dissenters. *In the Forest* fictionalizes the murder of Imelda Riney, her young son Liam and the priest, Father Joe Walsh, by Brendan O'Donnell in 1994, in County Clare. The 1990s trilogy 'got away with' addressing issues surrounding contemporary Ireland through reference to actual events, but on this occasion O'Brien's choice of focus has been condemned, by Fintan O'Toole for one, as 'contain[ing] an element of direct intrusion'.[3] In the light of long-standing assessments of O'Brien as a novelist whose primary concerns are personal rather than political, it is significant that O'Toole denies the 'public meaning' of the murders.

For me the real strength of *In the Forest* is the clarity with which O'Brien highlights the inextricable convergence of the personal and the political. Her dedication to the victims – 'In memoriam' – acknowledges the novel's basis in reality but she does address the 'bigger picture', analysing (as in her recent trilogy) the cultural contexts of the slayer and the slain. Although these contexts are indisputably Irish (and not just in terms of location), O'Brien does express wider-reaching concerns about the degree of nihilism and violence generated by existing social and symbolic orders.

In chapter 7 I argued that in concluding her trilogy on contemporary Ireland with the image of Breege 'holding it together', O'Brien was suggesting the need for revisions of these orders. *In the Forest* records the penalties incurred by a society which repeatedly denies this need. In this respect the novel represents far more than the simplistic 'return to Clare' which O'Toole sees as O'Brien's understandable if misguided response to a lengthy exile from her 'roots'. Pointing out that Ireland changed 'rapidly and profoundly' 'in the decades of her exile', O'Toole argues that O'Brien's 'need to avoid the trap of merely recycling the perceptions of the 1950s and 1960s has led her into an unusually direct approach to research', resulting in perceived intrusion upon private grief.

I feel conversely that O'Brien *deliberately* comes full circle, not 'recycling' but linking her original perceptions to the rural Ireland of the millennium. It is surely no coincidence that *In the Forest*'s murderous protagonist names his victim 'Catherine' and is termed a 'country boy' (*IF* 58, 168). Ronan Bennett comes close to identifying *In the Forest*'s power, pointing out that despite the 'crime stories' featured in the *Irish Times* 'on any day of the week', Ireland 'likes to think of itself as unlike anywhere in Europe' and that: 'It wants all the benefits of 21st-century success and, simultaneously, the social cohesion, neighbourliness and charitable impulses of a (half-imagined) past'.[4] O'Brien was revealing the extent to which this 'past' was 'half-imagined' back in 1960 when it was still 'present'. Again Bennett approaches the crux of this issue through his statement that *The Country Girls* trilogy addressed 'women's pleasures in a world where these went largely unacknowledged'. Cultures which deny the needs of half their members can only be 'half-imagined' at best, perhaps.

O'Brien's status as an established but not always closely heeded commentator on the position of women in the Republic of Ireland and beyond is highlighted by her decision to name the victim's sister 'Cassandra'.[5] Throughout *In the Forest* Cassandra experiences a sense of foreboding about her sister Eily, who has moved with her son Maddie to Cloosh Wood. Cassandra predicts that they 'won't stick it in the winter' and laments: *'Why did I ever let her bury herself in that strange old house with its haunted vibes?'* (*IF* 19, 68). When Eily and Maddie disappear, abducted by the murderer O'Kane, Cassandra – feeling 'cold, forewarned' – expresses her worries to the police and is initially ignored (*IF* 122). (The parallels between this incident and the original Cassandra's futile warnings of the fall and burning of Troy are highlighted by O'Brien's recurrent references to fire; O'Kane joyrides, then torches cars which he has feminized). It is significant that after the murder trial Cassandra is left standing 'outside time and place', reflecting not only the 'timeless' and universal aspects of the tragedy but the elusive nature of solutions (*IF* 203).

Despite *In the Forest*'s firm location within socio-historical context, its 'universality' continues to manifest itself in O'Brien's treatment of Eily Ryan and Mich O'Kane as archetypes – a device which in no way detracts from the humanity of the original victims and perpetrator, but which places the murders within a continuum of nihilism which, as O'Brien has been suggesting for over forty years, is the inevitable outcome of our unreconstituted social and symbolic orders. Thus Eily Ryan is translated variously into goddess, 'witch' (*IF* 90) and 'Madonna' (*IF* 39), whilst O'Kane is demonized as *Kinderschrek*.[6] O'Kane becomes the *locus* and projection of evil which the local community likes to conceptualize as 'out there'. But O'Kane is originally a local lad, a 'country boy' brutalized by violence, rejection and sexual abuse from the priest who was supposed to care for him. The community's implication in the development of 'country boy' into 'Kinderschrek' is highlighted by O'Brien's ongoing concentration on constructions of 'masculinity'. Eily's son Maddie is shown learning 'masculinity' at a children's party:

> they fought, rival gangs, *Bang bang, you're dead, I'm not dead*, up and down the wobbly stairs, into the garden, up in the trees, peeing on one another, Kevin squirting the girls with his water pistol . . . (*IF* 68)

Destroying the birthday girl's doll, Maddie becomes 'the baddie that hacked Hilda' for an ironically prophetic moment in which his own masculine identity collides and converges with O'Kane's (*IF* 71).

O'Kane is conflated in turn with the 'Jesus types' for whom Eily confesses a 'penchant' (*IF* 41). Raving as he marches Eily and Maddie to their deaths, he suggests collusion between himself and Christ:

> You won't see me losing the plot. Poor Jesus, poor fucker he lost the plot. Number one bloke. Him and me we did the odd gig. (*IF* 94)

After the murders, O'Kane's antics in prison earn him the nickname of 'Jumping Jesus' (*IF* 195). Any incongruity between this and 'Kinderschrek' is negated by O'Brien's reference to 'Jesus types' as 'shadow men'. Recalling the saint-like but lethal 'shadow males' of her early fiction and Baba's observation that God and Jesus hate women, this highlights the ongoing tenacity of the symbolic order.[7] Significantly, *In the Forest* depicts O'Kane as a child intoning the 'totem words' 'God hates me' (*IF* 4).

The perceived immutability of women's lot is confirmed by representations of Eily as construction and archetype. Her former lover Otto asks if he can paint her in triptych:

> first nude, the young Eily, vibrant, hungry, her burning hair . . . next she is older . . . a little belly on her . . . mother of three in a chemise and last a pilgrim woman going up a winding road (*IF* 39).

The projected vision of Eily as 'triple Goddess' (maiden, mother, crone) concurs with her expressed desire to 'get back to nature' and to achieve 'harmony' with the woodland (*IF* 26, 42).[8] The potentially empowering nature of this construction is, however, undermined by explicit connections between Otto and O'Kane. The murderer's childhood vision of 'a princess float[ing] by' in the woods anticipates Otto's 'conjur[ing]' of 'Chagall's floating angels circling above our valley' (*IF* 4, 39). Otto's language recalls that of Yeats, declaring his supposedly exclusive insight into Maud Gonne's 'pilgrim soul' in 'When You Are Old'. This in turn recalls O'Brien's use of intertextuality to reveal male domination of women and landscape in (for example) *A Pagan Place, Night* and *The High Road. In the Forest* echoes *The High Road* in its treatment within the context of landscape of the marginalization of relationships between women under patriarchy; Eily first discovers her affinity with woodland through the development of her friendship with

Madge. The women meet when Eily requests exhibition space at Madge's café for her drawings of nude women, 'many [of whom] were pregnant with proud voluptuous bellies' (*IF* 41).[9] The regenerative potential of this relationship is confirmed by the women's mutual 'pledge to be always there for one another', but this is sidelined by Eily's subsequent relationship with Sven (*IF* 42). Her break-up with Sven precipitates her relocation to Cloosh Wood.

In keeping with her fatal choice of alignment with the masculine, Eily's chosen space has already been appropriated by O'Kane, who identifies himself with the woods and who as a child '[gave] himself a secret name, Caoilte, the name of the forests' (*IF* 4). Within the context of the forest, Eily is eerily linked with O'Kane's own mother and also with the mother of God. O'Kane's early development has been skewed by the sight of his dead mother, 'lying on a slab with no colour in her cheeks and no breath' in snowy weather; he becomes convinced that this Sleeping Beauty/Snow White figure has been buried alive. Eily and Maddie try desperately to distract O'Kane with fairytales as he leads them deeper into the inevitably archetypal forest, where they happen upon 'a glass casket with the figure of the Virgin Mary, such as [Eily] has seen on roadside shrines' (*IF* 105, 110). O'Kane's response to this figure – 'Fuck you Our Lady' – presages the murder of Eily herself. Ironically, a detective investigating the scene later marvels that 'these shrines are never harmed' (*IF* 181).

O'Kane himself demonstrates a warped but fervent respect for maternity, insisting even after the murder upon the 'sacred' nature of the 'bond' between 'mother and child' (*IF* 131). His antithetical responses and behaviour are explained through the reflections of Maddie's father at the funeral:

> Herself and the child were one, indivisible, and O'Kane, the outcast, had seen that and had wanted it and had had to destroy it in his hunger to belong. (*IF* 189).

Echoing earlier references to the commonality of 'masculinity', the father's 'estrange[ment]' is implicitly linked to the alienation of O'Kane.

As in (for example) *House of Splendid Isolation*, the phenomenon of cultural matricide is explored through O'Brien's deployment of 'egg' imagery. Following the instructions of a female friend, Eily and Maddie decorate eggs for Easter. What should be a celebration of 'fertility' is rendered nihilistic by the presence of O'Kane, spying from his hideout in the forest. Maddie is overcome with revulsion for the blown egg white, which he says is 'yukky'; this later becomes his term for O'Kane (IF 65, 66, 94). Eily's death is anticipated by the image of the 'painted eggs' looking 'as if they might be shattered into smithereens', and later by the 'lovely' wardrobe which O'Kane 'smashe[s] in', stealing the gun which becomes the murder weapon (IF 74). The wardrobe container becomes a symbol of the mother's insides.[10]

The implications of constructing cultures and societies on matricide are most poignantly clarified by the novel's climactic conflation of 'mothers'. The sight of Maddie 'screaming over a dead mother' recalls O'Kane's own loss; Eily at the moment of her death becomes a sacrificial cipher for 'all womankind' (IF 171, 113). Later O'Kane has a vision of Eily with his mother in the woods (IF 113, 208). Eily appears with 'drops of blood' 'run[ning] down her face' from her shot eye; her iconic status is compounded by her striking resemblance to a weeping statue.[11] Her own mother sits through the trial 'with the stillness of an archetype' (IF 209).

During O'Kane's trial, his counsel says that:

> the young man did not deserve to stand there alone because the country itself was on trial, it had failed him, the system had failed him as from the age of ten he was shuttled from one institution to another, motherless, fatherless ... (IF 201)

In the light of Fintan O'Toole's attempts to 'depoliticize' the murders, this is a deeply revealing speech. O'Kane is hardly isolated in 'motherlessness'; 'the country itself' – ironically feminized as 'Mother Ireland' – must always be 'motherless' under matricidal orders.

O'Brien has progressed over forty-two years from her tentative explorations of cultural matricide through the death of Mrs Brady and sterilization of Kate, to a sophisticated indictment of social and symbolic orders which continue to construct their women as 'Madonna' or 'witch'. Edna O'Brien is a 'Cassandra' for our time.

Notes

CHAPTER 1. EDNA O'BRIEN AND HER CRITICS

1. Grace Eckley, *Edna O'Brien* (Cranbury: New Jersey, Associated University Presses, 1974), 9.
2. Guardian, 2 October 1999.
3. Rebecca Pelan, 'Edna O'Brien's "Stage-Irish" Persona: An "Act" of Resistance', in the *Canadian Journal of Irish Studies* (henceforth *CJIS*), 19:1 (1993), 67–78.
4. Charles Nevin, 'Captain Moonlight: The Grave's a Fine and Public Place', *Independent* (30 January 1994), 26.
5. Julia Carlson (ed.), *Banned in Ireland: Censorship and the Irish Writer* (London: Routledge, 1990), 73.
6. Joan Smith, 'Tears and Terrors in the Wind', *Independent*, 24 April 1994, 33.
7. *Independent*, 5 October 1995.
8. Fintan O'Toole, 'Come off it, Gerry, Larry – and Edna', *Guardian*, 2 February 1994, 20; Edward Pearce, 'Words with No Wisdom', *Guardian* 12 July 1994, 18.
9. O'Brien is recurrently constructed in relation to Lessing; Godwin is echoing not only the National Portrait Gallery but Sheila Rowbotham, who in her commentary on the position of women in the 1960s refers to 'novels [of the period] which explored how to be women, from Doris Lessing's lust and autonomy to Edna O'Brien's romance and abandonment' (*A Century of Women* (London: Viking, 1997), 338).
10. See Nicholas Wroe, 'Country Matters', *Guardian*, 2 October 1999, 6–7.
11. Andrew Duncan, 'The Andrew Duncan Interview', *Radio Times*, 23 September 1994, 26–8.
12. Ann Chisholm, 'Looking for Trouble', *Sydney Morning Herald*, 24 September 1994, 10.

13. O'Brien was herself well aware of the risks inherent in addressing 'the troubles', commenting: 'The idea is that this is the big boys' turf ... Well, tough'. See Mick Brown, 'The Sweet One Gets Angry', *Daily Telegraph*, 24 September 1994, 21.

14. Chisholm, 'Looking for Trouble', 10.

15. Angela Lambert, 'May All Her Sins Now Be Forgiven', *Daily Mail*, 16 April 1994, 22.

16. Emer Kelly, 'This Country Girl Is Not a Real Woman', *Sunday Independent*, 3 October 1999, 11.

17. Maureen L. Grogan, 'Using Memory and Adding Emotion: The (Re)Creation of Experience in the Short Fiction of Edna O'Brien', in *CJIS: Special Edition on Edna O'Brien*, 22:2 (1996), 9–20.

18. Eckley, *Edna O'Brien*, 14.

19. Ibid.

20. Peggy O'Brien, 'The Silly and the Serious: An Assessment of Edna O'Brien', in *Massachusetts Review*, 28 (1987). 474–88.

21. Ibid., 483.

22. Darcy O'Brien, 'Edna O'Brien: A Kind of Irish Childhood', in Thomas Staley (ed.), *Twentieth-Century Women Novelists* (London: Macmillan, 1982), 179–90.

23. See Shusha Guppy, 'Interview with Edna O'Brien', in *Paris Review*, 92 (1984), 22–50.

24. Jeanette Winterson, Introduction, in *Oranges Are Not the Only Fruit* (1985; London: Vintage, 1996), xi–xv.

25. Toril Moi, *Simone de Beauvoir: The Making of an Intellectual Woman* (Oxford: Blackwell, 1994), 5.

26. Mary Salmon, 'Edna O'Brien', in *Contemporary Irish Novelists*, ed. Rudiger Imhof (Tübingen: Gunter Narr Verlag, 1990), 143–58.

27. Salmon, 'Edna O'Brien', 143.

28. Grogan, 'Using Memory and Adding Emotion',18.

29. Rebecca Pelan, 'Edna O'Brien's "World of Nora Barnacle" ', in *CJIS*, 22:2 (1996), 49–61.

30. Lorna Rooks-Hughes, 'The Family and the Female Body in the Novels of Edna O'Brien and Julia O'Faolain', in *CJIS*, 22:2 (1996), 83–98.

31. Dawn Duncan, 'Edna O'Brien and Virginia', in *CJIS*, 22:2 (1996), 99–106.

32. Kiera O'Hara, 'Love Objects: Love and Obsession in the Stories of Edna O'Brien', in *Studies in Short Fiction*, 30:3 (1983), 317–25.

33. Pelan, 'Edna O'Brien's "Stage-Irish" Persona', 76.

34. Janice Radway, *Reading the Romance: Patriarchy and Popular Literature* (London: Verso, 1987).

35. See Katie Gramich, 'God, Word and Nation: Language and

Religion in Works by V. S. Naipaul, Edna O'Brien and Emyr Humphries', in *Swansea Review*, 1994, 229–42.

36. Pelan, 'Edna O'Brien's "Stage-Irish" Persona', 77.
37. Sandra Manoogian Pearce, 'An Interview with Edna O'Brien', in *CJIS*, 22:2 (1996), 5–8.
38. Pelan, 'Edna O'Brien's "Stage-Irish" Persona', 78.

CHAPTER 2. EDNA O'BRIEN: 'IRISH WOMAN WRITER'

1. Gerry Smyth, 'Being Difficult: The Irish Writer in Britain', in *Eire-Ireland*, Fall / Winter 1996, 41–57.
2. Gerry Smyth, 'Being Difficult', 41.
3. Ibid., 47.
4. Ibid.
5. Ibid., 49.
6. Ibid., 52–3.
7. Patricia Boyle Haberstroh, *Women Creating Women: Contemporary Irish Women Poets* (New York: Syracuse University Press, 1996), 4.
8. Ibid., 4–5.
9. Ibid., 9.
10. Mary O'Connor, 'The Thieves of Language in Gaol?', in *Krino*, 15 (Spring 1994), 30–42.
11. It is interesting to note O'Brien's own comment on the issue of 'persona'; in an interview with Susha Guppy she speculated on whether she has received 'more serious consideration in the United States than in Britain' 'because [she is] not known there as a "personality"'!'
12. Julia Carlson (ed.), *Banned in Ireland: Censorship and the Irish Writer* (London: Routledge, 1990), 73.
13. Claudia Pattison, 'Edna's Stock-in-Trade', *Western Mail*, 25 April 1994, 8.
14. O'Brien's eyes are blue. Recurrent perceptions of their 'greenness' – which reinforce O'Brien's 'Irishness' – seem to have been generated by *Girl with Green Eyes*, the film version of *The Lonely Girl*, starring Rita Tushingham.
15. Julie Burchill, *Guardian Weekend*, 2 October 1999, 3.
16. Emer Kelly, 'This Country Girl Is Not a Real Woman', *Sunday Independent*, 3 October 1999, 11.
17. Rebecca Pelan, 'Edna O'Brien's "Stage-Irish" Persona: An "Act" of Resistance', in *CJIS*, 9:1 (1993), 68.
18. *August is a Wicked Month* and *Casualties of Peace* were published in 1965 and 1966 respectively. These novels signalled a major

departure from the *Country Girls* trilogy, abandoning the Irish setting and encompassing between them sado-masochism, murder and venereal disease. Sean MacMahon commented in 1967 that 'Miss O'Brien seem[s] in places to be writing a kind of neo-feminist propoganda'.

19. Pelan, 'Edna O'Brien's "Stage-Irish" Persona', 70. I shall argue later that the 'neo-feminist propoganda' is in fact the subtext of *The Country Girls*, and that *August is a Wicked Month* and *Casualties of Peace* develop, rather than depart from, the earlier texts.

20. O'Brien's books were banned in Southern Ireland by the National Censorship Board; censorship became law in 1929 when the Censorship of Publications Act was passed. Julia Carlson summarizes the Act's criteria for banning publications; these include material perceived as 'indecent' or 'obscene'; 'indecent' 'is defined "as including suggestive of, or inciting to sexual immorality or unnatural vice or likely in any other similar way to corrupt or deprave" ' (Carlson, *Banned in Ireland*, 4). Any apparent advocation of contraception was also seen as grounds for censorship. Carlson highlights the 'paternalism' of the board and points out that: 'Although the Censorship Board is required to take into consideration, among other things, "the literary, artistic, scientific or historic merit or importance" and "the class of reader . . . which may reasonably be expected to read such a book or edition", the board is answerable only to the minister for justice, not to a wider public'.

21. Edna O'Brien, *Mother Ireland* (London: Weidenfeld and Nicolson, 1976), 11.

22. Ailbhe Smyth, 'The Floozie in the Jacuzzi: Intertextual Inserts', in *Irish Review*, 6:7–24.

23. Ibid., 14.

24. C. L. Innes, *Women and Nation in Irish Literature and Society, 1880–1935* (London: Harvester Wheatsheaf, 1993), 15.

25. Innes, *Women and Nation*, 9.

26. Ibid., 2.

27. Ibid., 3.

28. Pelan, 'Edna O'Brien's "Stage-Irish" Persona'.

29. Innes, *Women and Nation*, 38.

30. Ibid., 41–2.

31. Ibid., 4.

32. Haberstroh notes that: 'Isolated examples can be found to illustrate Yeats's support for writers like Kathleen Tynan and Dorothy Wellesley, but that support is sometimes patronizing. At the end of the year in which she first met Yeats, Dorothy

Wellesley reports: "W. B. Y. is for ever trying to revise my poems. We have quarrelled about this. I say to him: 'I prefer bad poems written by myself to good poems written by you under my name" ' (Haberstroh, *Women Creating Women*, 3).

33. Innes, *Women and Nation*, 4.
34. Pelan, 'Edna O'Brien's "Stage-Irish" Persona', 75, 72.
35. Ibid., 77.
36. Catherine Nash, 'Reclaiming Vision: Looking at Landscape and the Body', in *Gender, Place and Culture*, 3:4 (1996), 149.

CHAPTER 3. NEGATIVE ROMANCE AND GLACIAL NIHILISM: THE 1960s

1. Angela Lambert, 'May All her Sins Now Be Forgiven', *Daily Mail*, 16 April 1994, 22.
2. In *Girl with Green Eyes* and *Girls in their Married Bliss* Caithleen's name is anglicized by her lover / husband Eugene to 'Kate'. In this chapter I shall refer to 'Caithleen' or 'Kate' according to the text being discussed.
3. Julia Carlson, *Banned in Ireland: Censorship and the Irish Writer* (London:Routledge, 1990), 73.
4. Liz Heron, *Truth, Dare or Promise: Girls Growing Up in the Fifties* (London: Virago, 1985), 3.
5. Bernice Schrank and Danine Farquharson, 'Object of Love, Subject to Despair: Edna O'Brien's *The Love Object* and the Emotional Logic of Late Romanticism', in *CJIS*, 22:2 (1996), 21.
6. Friedan, Betty, *The Feminine Mystique* (1963; Harmondsworth: Penguin, 1965), 68.
7. Ibid., 293.
8. Rebecca Pelan, 'Edna O'Brien's "Stage-Irish" Persona: An "Act" of Resistance', in *CJIS*, 19:1 (1993), 73.
9. Germaine Greer, *The Female Eunuch* (1970; London: Granada, 1981), 102.
10. Macleod, Sheila, 'A Fairy Story', in Sara Maitland (ed.), *Very Heaven: Looking Back at the 1960s* (London: Virago, 1988), 181–2.
11. Pelan, 'Edna O'Brien's "Stage-Irish" Persona', 69.
12. Peggy O'Brien, 'The Silly and the Serious: An Assessment of Edna O'Brien', in *Massachusetts Review*, 28 (1987), 484.
13. Interestingly there was a rococo-influenced Art Nouveau artist and furniture designer called Eugene Gaillard; O'Brien's deployment of this name reinforces the impact of his 'designs' on Kate. Significantly, when Kate leaves his home at the end of *Girl with*

Green Eyes she realizes that she has 'contributed nothing . . . not even a cushion' to his domestic interior (*GGE* 189).

14. Coward, Rosalind, 'Female Desire: Women's Sexuality Today', in *Feminist Literary Theory: A Reader*, ed. Mary Eagleton (Oxford: Blackwell, 1986), 145–8.

15. Janice Radway, *Reading the Romance: Patriarchy and Popular Literature* (London: Verso, 1987), 64.

16. It must be admitted though that Martha, the protagonist of 'The Love Object', is herself objectified. Though, as an act of resistance to 'femininity' she 'never buy[s] cleaning stuffs' but 'just throw[s] things away', she remains susceptible to commodities such as 'bottles of scent and beautiful clothes' and proves ultimately to be a throwaway commodity for her lover. Furthermore her professional life as a 'television announcer' is significantly sidelined throughout the narrative.

17. Linda Hutcheon, *The Politics of Postmodernism* (London: Routledge, 1989), 13.

18. Grace Eckley, *Edna O'Brien* (Cranbury: New Jersey, Associated University Presses, 1974), 25.

19. Caithleen is eating Turkish delight and eyeing up Mr Gentleman at a performance of *East Lynne* while her mother is supposedly drowned when rowing with her lover on the Shannon lake. This is significant since Mrs Brady is in Irigarayan terms culturally 'murdered' and *East Lynne* is itself an indicator of disruption at the heart of the domestic idyll.

20. Sonya Andermahr, Terry Lovell and Carol Wolkowitz, *A Concise Glossary of Feminist Theory* (London: Arnold, 1997), 137.

21. Tania Modleski, *Loving with a Vengeance: Mass-Produced Fantasies for Women* (London: Methuen, 1982), 79.

22. In Mary Eagleton (ed.), *Feminist Literary Theory: A Reader* (Oxford: Blackwell, 1986), 43.

23. Ibid., 136.

24. This recalls the episode in Rebecca where the second Mrs de Winter borrows Rebecca's mackintosh and finds a monogrammed handkerchief inside the pocket:

I must have been the first person to put on that mackintosh since the handkerchief was used. She who wore it was tall, slim, broader than me about the shoulders, for I had found it big and overlong, and the sleeves had come below my wrist. (Du Maurier, Rebecca (1938; London: Arrow, 1992), 125).

25. Modleski, *Loving with a Vengeance*, 60, 79.

26. Radway, *Reading the Romance*, 151.

27. Eckley, *Edna O'Brien*, 78

28. Radway, *Reading the Romance*, 117.
29. O'Brien, 'The Silly and the Serious', 484.
30. 'Paradise' is interesting in that it continues the 'drowning' metaphor introduced in *The Country Girls*, which recurs throughout O'Brien's fiction. The protagonist, initially fearful of water, learns to swim and at the end of the story almost succeeds in drowning herself, experiencing in the process 'a great beautiful bountiful baptism' (*LO* 234). In chapter 6, I shall argue with reference to *The High Road* that the drowning metaphor indicates the incompatibility of socially constructed 'femininity' with the female body and 'unstable' fluids identified by Irigaray. The protagonist's submission to water is of course also relevant to O'Brien's later work on Virginia Woolf , which I shall address in chapter 4.
31. Judith Butler, 'Performative Acts and Gender Constitution: An Essay in Phenomenology and Feminist Theory', in Katie Conboy, Nadia Medina and Sarah Stanbury (eds), *Writing on the Body: Female Embodiment and Feminist Theory* (New York: Columbia University Press, 1997), 403. In the context of Ellen's response to the drag act, Angela Carter's alignment of O'Brien with Jean Rhys is significant. Carter argues that both are 'women writers [who] pretend to be female impersonators . . . [and] whose scars glorify the sex that wounds them' (Angela Carter, *Shaking a Leg: Collected Journalism and Writing*, ed. Jenny Uglow (London: Vintage, 1998), 499). Carter's identification of O'Brien as a 'female impersonator' suggests that she is aware of O'Brien's engagement with social constructions of 'femininity'.
32. Irigaray, Luce, *Je, Tu, Nous: Toward a Culture of Difference*, trans. Alison Martin (London: Routledge, 1993).
33. *Casualties of Peace* is dedicated to 'Rita Tushingham whose coat it is'. This is significant given that Tushingham played Kate in *Girl with Green Eyes* and that Auro is a cameraman who 'frames' women.
34. Mary Salmon, 'Edna O'Brien', in Rudiger Imhof (ed.), *Contemporary Irish Novelists* (Tübingen: Gunter Narr Verlag, 1990), 147.
35. Rebecca Pelan, 'Edna O'Brien's "World of Nora Barnacle"', in *CJIS*, 22:2 (1996), 53.
36. Carlson, *Banned in Ireland*, 76. *The Country Girls* was banned under the Censorship of Publications Act of 1929, which as Carlson records 'reflects the moral concerns and principles of the leaders of the [then] new Irish Free State', 'provid[ing] for the banning of publications' on the grounds of, for example, perceived indecency or obscenity. 'Indecent' 'is defined "as including suggestive of, or inciting to sexual immorality or unnatural vice or likely in any

other similar way to corrupt or deprave" ' (pp. 3–4). In this context O'Brien's self-confessed representations of 'Irish girls full of yearnings and desires' subvert national and cultural constructions of 'femininity'.

37. In *The Country Girls* Cait and Baba recite 'Lord Ullin's Daughter' together on their way home from their first night out in Dublin. The poem itself is a lament for lost innocence:

From a Munster vale they brought her
From the pure and balmy air,
An Ormond Ullin's daughter
With blue eyes and golden hair.
They brought her to the city
And she slowly faded there,
For consumption has no pity
For blue eyes and golden hair.

Significantly Baba herself later becomes consumptive.

38. Throughout this study I address 'Joyce' not as a writer or personality but as O'Brien's literary 'father'. I do not set out to engage in Joycean criticism since my aim is to demonstrate that, regardless of whether or not O'Brien's pastiche of Joyce is deployed in a spirit of homage and/or arising from stylistic and cultural dependence, it does symbolize her entrapment as an Irish woman writer.

CHAPTER 4. 'WOMAN MUST WRITE HERSELF': *A PAGAN PLACE* AND *NIGHT*

1. In chapter 1, I acknowledged the problematics of 'French feminism' as an umbrella term. In this chapter I shall refer principally to Irigaray, having deployed her work on 'femininity' and 'the market' in readings of O'Brien's 1960s texts, and to Cixous, whose identification of the necessity for *écriture feminine* is clearly relevant to *Night*. Cixous does seem to carry a certain resonance for Irish women writers; Eavan Boland, for example, admits to being 'haunted' by 'The Laugh of the Medusa' (E. Boland, *Object Lessons: The Life of the Woman and the Poet in Our Time* (London: Vintage, 1996), 125). Bonnie Lynne Davies has identified O'Brien with Cixous, arguing that 'both identif[y] language as gendered and ... describ[e] woman as imprisoned and disadvantaged by patriarchal discourse' ('Re-Constructing the Brick Wall of Phallocentric Discourse: Nell Finds Her M(Other) Tongue in Edna O'Brien's *Time and Tide*', in *CJIS*, 22:2 (1996) 73).

Ecofeminism is 'a holistic approach to all forms of domination – sex, race [and] species' which 'is more than a manifesto [since] it already lives in the actions of all women' (Ariel Salleh, *Ecofeminism as Politics: Nature, Marx and the Postmodern* (London: Zed Books, 1997), 109, xiv). In this sense ecofeminism can offer significant insights into O'Brien's processes of 'recovery'.

2. Joseph Bristow, *Sexuality* (London: Routledge, 1997), 85–6.
3. In Mary Eagleton (ed.), *Feminist Literary Theory: A Reader* (Oxford: Blackwell, 1986), 221. For an illuminating analysis of the liberatory potential for Irish women of *écriture feminine*, see Ailbhe Smyth's 'The Floozie in the Jacuzzi': Intertextual Inserts', in *Irish Review*, 6 (1989), 7–24. Taking as her title a colloquial name for the statue of Joyce's Anna Livia (a feminization of the River Liffey) in Dublin's O'Connell Street, Smyth celebrates 'ANNA LIVIA PLURABILITY / *The Singular Diversities and Diverse Singularities of Irish Women*' ('The Floozie in the Jacuzzi', 7).
4. In Elaine Marks and Isabelle de Courtivron (eds), *New French Feminisms: An Anthology* (Brighton: Harvester Press, 1981), 245.
5. C. L. Innes, *Women and Nation in Irish Literature and Society, 1880–1935* (London: Harvester Wheatsheaf, 1993), 3.
6. Ibid., 4.
7. See, for example, Terry Eagleton in M. Eagleton (ed.), *Feminist Literary Theory*, 214–15.
8. In Marks and de Courtivron (eds), *New French Feminisms*, 246. Andermahr, Lovell and Wolkowitz explain Cixous's concept of 'the imaginary' as 'women's spiritual and linguistic home, a place which exists prior to masculine law and where female creativity is spontaneously expressed' (Sonya Andermahr, Terry Lovell and Carol Wolkowitz, *A Concise Glossary of Feminist Theory* (London: Arnold, 1997), 60).
9. See *Times Literary Supplement*, 6 October 1972.
10. See Margaret Whitford, *Luce Irigaray: Philosophy in the Feminine* (London: Routledge, 1991), 49.
11. Julia Carlson (ed.), *Banned in Ireland: Censorship and the Irish Writer* (London: Routledge, 1990), 75–6.
12. Cheryl Herr, 'The Erotics of Irishness', in *Critical Inquiry*, 17:1 (Autumn 1990), 1–34; Carlson (ed.), *Banned in Ireland*, 75.
13. Rebecca Pelan, 'Edna O'Brien's "World of Nora Barnacle" ', in the *CJIS*, 22:2, 1996, 49.
14. Ibid., 51.
15. See *Je, Tu, Nous* (London: Routledge, 1993), 23.
16. This episode very specifically realizes 'the world of Nora Barnacle'; in *James Joyce* O'Brien records that Joyce told his brother

Stanislaus 'some of [Barnacle's] most precious secrets, her early cavorts, a near seduction by a young curate . . . a thrashing from an uncle which developed into some kind of orgasmic fit' (*JJ* 45).

17. Margaret Whitford (ed.), *The Irigaray Reader* (Oxford: Blackwell, 1991), 92.

18. Mary Jacobus, *First Things: The Maternal Imaginary in Literature, Art and Psychoanalysis* (London: Routledge, 1995), 6–7.

19. Innes, *Women and Nation*, 221.

20. See *Je, Tu, Nous*, 26. Irigaray asks: 'If God is always imagined to be a father, how can women find in Him a model of identity?' (Whitford, *Luce Irigaray*, 112). The *Pagan Place* narrator seems to explore this question.

21. I use 'paternal law' to encompass not only the Lacanian 'Law of the Father' which as Andermahr, Lovell and Wolcowitz point out 'refers to that set of psychosexual injunctions . . . which constitute the symbolic order', but 'the law of . . . all fathers: fathers of families, fathers of nations, religious fathers, professor-fathers doctor-fathers, lover-fathers, etc.', which Irigaray identifies as perpetrating cultural matricide. Irigaray's concept of 'the law of the father' highlights the patriarchal construction common to symbolic 'law' and legislation; in this respect her arguments are pertinent to Southern Irish women subject not only to cultural imperialism but to rigorous laws regarding (for example) abortion. See *A Concise Glossary of Feminist Theory*, 121; Whitford, *Luce Irigaray*, 36.

22. Innes, *Women and Nation*, 41. Asked by Julia Carlson: 'What kind of image of woman do you think people wish to see in Ireland?' O'Brien replied: 'The pedestal image; devoid of sexual desires, maternal, devout, attractive. Quite a handful!' O'Brien is clearly aware of the intrinsic connection between 'patriarchal authority' and constructions of Mary as asexual.

23. This echoes 'The Dead' from Joyce's *Dubliners*, a text to which O'Brien will refer throughout her work.

24. In 'The Bodily Encounter with the Mother' Irigaray argues that the Oedipus complex forbids desires for the mother and indeed that: 'The social order, our culture, psychoanalysis itself wants it this way; the mother must remain forbidden, excluded' (Whitford, *Luce Irigaray*, 39).

25 Ariel Salleh argues that 'Under the [patriarchal] Eurocentric regime, all discourses become property systems, ways of dividing up matter and suppressing the amniotic flow of lived time' (Salleh, *Ecofeminism as Politics*, 190).

26 See Irigaray, 'And the One Doesn't Stir Without the Other', in *Signs*, 7:1 (Autumn 1981), 60–67.

27 See Irigaray in Whitford, *Luce Irigaray*, 124.

28 Dawn Duncan, 'Edna O'Brien and *Virginia*', in *CJIS*, 22:2 (1996), 101

29 Rebecca Pelan, 'Edna O'Brien's "World of Nora Barnacle" ', in *CJIS*, 22:2 (1996), 59.

30. Sandra Manoogian Pearce, 'Redemption through Reconciliation: Edna O'Brien's Isolated Women', in *CJIS*, 22:2 (1996), 64. The title poem from Yeats's 1919 collection *The Wild Swans at Coole* features fifty-nine 'mysterious, beautiful' swans.

31. See Innes, *Women and Nation*, 21.

32. Pelan, 'Edna O'Brien's "World of Nora Barnacle" ', 58.

33. The falconer also echoes Yeats, whose poem 'The Second Coming' opens:
     Turning and turning in the widening gyre
     The falcon cannot hear the falconer . . .
     O'Brien's falconer significantly fails to achieve a 'second coming'.

34. Innes identifies 'dark Rosaleen' as a male construction of a feminized Ireland, citing James Clarence Mangan's ballad of that name (Innes, *Women and Nation*, 21).

35. Whitford (ed.), *The Irigaray Reader*, 105.

36. In fact Shakespeare is not O'Brien's only antecedent here, though he is the only one directly acknowledged; as Innes points out 'the struggle for authority played out by father / son figures is one that recurs almost obsessively in Irish drama and fiction' (Innes, *Women and Nation*, 48).

37. Whitford (ed.), *The Irigaray Reader*, 105.

38. Irigaray, 'And the One Doesn't Stir Without the Other', 62.

39. Whitford (ed.), *The Irigaray Reader*, 136.

CHAPTER 5. 'ANOTHER BIRTH': *MOTHER IRELAND* AND *VIRGINIA*

1. O'Brien collaborated in the production of *Mother Ireland* with the photographer Fergus Bourke; she acknowledges the centrality of his work to the text by stressing in the acknowledgements that 'only half the book' is her doing. I shall analyse the 'picturesque' nature of Bourke's representations, and their relevance to representations of O'Brien herself, later in this chapter. In the light of Cheryl Herr's analysis of cultural 'stilling' in Ireland (I cited Herr's commentary on the suppression of *écriture feminine* in Ireland in the last chapter) the use of photography to represent 'mother country' is significant. Herr argues that:

Ireland has literally eroded, in the sphere of representations that constitute social identity, a comfortable sense of the body; in traditional as well as in colonial and postcolonial Ireland, the body has frequently been associated representationally with danger and scrutinised with an intensity that *stills* (photographically). (Cheryl Herr, 'The Erotics of Irishness', in *Critical Inquiry*, 17:1 (1990), 6–7)

2. See Judith Butler, 'Performative Acts and Gender Constitution: An Essay in Phenomenology and Feminist Theory', in Katie Conroy, Nadia Medina and Sarah Stanbury (eds), *Writing on the Body: Female Embodiment and Feminist Theory* (New York: Columbia University Press, 1997), 402.

3. Toril Moi, *Simone de Beauvoir: The Making of and Intellectual Woman* (Oxford: Blackwell, 1994), 5.

4. See Maureen Grogan, 'Using Memory and Adding Emotion: The (Re)Creation of Experience in the Short Fiction of Edna O'Brien', in *CJIS*, 22:2 (1996), 9–20.

5. It is easy to identify throughout *Mother Ireland* events which have already featured in the novels as well as in the short stories, for example the narrator's move from the rural west to Dublin, and thence to England. But it is not my aim to elaborate on these parallels, which are readily identifiable by any reader of O'Brien's work.

6. Moi, *Simone de Beauvoir*, 5.

7. Eavan Boland, *Object Lessons: The Life of the Woman and the Poet in Our Time* (London: Vintage, 1996), 103.

8. I refer throughout this chapter to 'the narrator' or 'Edna' – keeping the inverted commas – in recognition of textual ambiguities and to distinguish the various 'I's and 'you's of the text from O'Brien herself.

9. Rebecca Pelan, 'Edna O'Brien's "World of Nora Barnacle" ', in *CJIS*, 22:2 (1996), 51.

10. Seamus Deane, *Strange Country: Modernity and Nationhood in Irish Writing since 1790* (Oxford: Oxford University Press, 1997), 89.

11. Peggy O'Brien, 'The Silly and the Serious: An Assessment of Edna O'Brien', in *Massachusetts Review*, 28 (1987), 475.

12. See Marina Warner, *Alone of All Her Sex: The Myth and the Cult of the Virgin Mary* (London: Weidenfeld and Nicolson, 1976). Coincidentally published in the same year and by the same publisher as *Mother Ireland*, this gives a fascinating account of shifting cultural perceptions of 'Mary'; Warner's analysis of the Virgin's role in the Catholic societies of Southern Ireland and the Mediterranean is especially pertinent to O'Brien's work.

13. See Luce Irigaray, 'And the One Doesn't Stir Without the Other', *Signs*, 7:1 (1981), 60–67.
14. Chaia Heller, 'For the Love of Nature: Ecology and the Cult of the Romantic', in Greta Gaard (ed.), *Ecofeminism: Women, Animals, Nature* (Philadelphia: Temple University Press, 1993), 221. In the light of O'Brien's increasing concern for the 'maternal body' of the land – for environmental issues – it is significant that Heller is discussing constructions of 'mother Earth' / Gaia as a 'damsel in distress'. In *The High Road* (1988) O'Brien's environmentalism extends beyond Ireland.
15. Herr, Cheryl, 'The Erotics of Irishness', in *Critical Inquiry*, 17:1 (Autumn 1990), 8.
16. See Ailbhe Smyth, 'The Floozie in the Jacuzzi: Intertextual Inserts', in *Irish Review*, 6 (1989), 7–24.
17. Here O'Brien seems once more to be anticipating the zeitgeist; in recent criticism the dangers inherent in culture / nature dualism in relation to Ireland have been succinctly expressed by Gerry Smyth, whose answer to the question of 'What is the most pressing issue in Irish Studies today?' is 'Sellafield Nuclear Reprocessing Plant' ('Irish Studies, Postcolonial Theory and the "New" Essentialism', *Irish Studies Review*, 7:2 (1999), 218).
18. See Luce Irigaray, 'This Sex Which Is Not One', in *This Sex Which Is Not One*, trans. Catherine Porter (Ithaca: Cornell University Press, 1985), 23–33.
19. Mary Jacobus, *First Things: The Maternal Imaginary in Literature, Art and Psychoanalysis* (London: Routledge, 1995), 20.
20. Ibid., 1–2.
21. For an incisive analysis of O'Brien's relationship to Woolf, see Dawn Duncan, 'Edna O'Brien and Virginia', in *CJIS*, 22:2 (1996), 99–106.
22. Duncan, 'Edna O'Brien and Virginia', 99.
23. Clare Hanson, ' "As a Woman I Have No Country": Woolf and the Construction of National Identity', in Tracey Hill and William Hughes (eds), *Contemporary Writing and National Identity* (Bath: Sulis Press, 1995).
24. Ibid., 54.
25. Ibid., 62–3.
26. Drowning is a recurrent theme in O'Brien's fiction. Mrs Brady drowns in *The Country Girls*; a child drowns in *The High Road* (1988), and in the significantly titled *Time and Tide* (1992) the protagonist's son drowns in a Thames ferry disaster.

CHAPTER 6. 'AN OTHER LANDSCAPE': *THE HIGH ROAD*

1. See Sandra Manoogian Pearce, 'An Interview with Edna O'Brien', in *CJIS*, 22:2 (1996), 5–8.
2. See Luce Irigaray, 'The Bodily Encounter with the Mother', in *The Irigaray Reader*, ed. Margaret Whitford (Oxford: Blackwell, 1991), 34–46.
3. In the context of the nuclear family as a microcosm of capitalism, it is worth noting Irigaray's claim that contemporary *jouissance* 'is in fact basically capitalist [since] it is an appropriation-exploitation of the bodies of women-mothers'. See 'Women-Mothers, the Silent Substratum of the Social Order', in Whitford *The Irigaray Reader*, (ed.), 47–52.
4. See Luce Irigaray, 'Women on the Market', in *This Sex Which Is Not One*, trans. Catherine Porter (Ithaca: Cornell University Press, 1985), 170–91.
5. See Luce Irigaray, 'The Bodily Encounter with the Mother'.
6. Pat O'Connor, *Friendships Between Women: A Critical Review* (Hemel Hempstead: Harvester Wheatsheaf, 1992), 182.
7. Christine St Peter, *Changing Ireland: Strategies in Contemporary Women's Fiction* (Basingstoke: Macmillan, 2000), 73.
8. Marina Warner, *Alone of All Her Sex: The Myth and the Cult of the Virgin Mary* (London: Weidenfeld and Nicolson, 1976), 183.
9. Seamus Deane, *Strange Country: Modernity and Nationhood in Irish Writing since 1790* (Oxford: Oxford University Press, 1997), 89.
10. See Luce Irigaray, *This Sex Which Is Not One*, trans. Catherine Porter (Ithaca: Cornell University Press, 1985), 186.
11. See Whitford (ed.), *The Irigaray Reader*, 92.
12. See Irigaray, *This Sex Which Is Not One*, 178. My interpretation of 'copying' is in this context that woman mimics patriarchal constructions of 'femininity' such as the Virgin.
13. See Elisabeth Brooke, *A Woman's Book of Shadows* (London: The Women's Press, 1993), 21.
14. Luce Irigaray, *Je, Tu, Nous: Toward a Culture of Difference*, trans. Alison Martin (London: Routledge, 1993), 173.
15. Jim Cheney, 'Nature / Theory / Difference: Ecofeminism and the Reconstruction of Environmental Ethics', in Karen Warren (ed.), *Ecological Feminism* (London: Routledge, 1994), 158–78.
16. Warren (ed.), *Ecological Feminism* (London: Routledge, 1994), 186.
17. See Patrick D. Murphy, *Literature, Nature and Other: Ecofeminist Critiques* (Albany: State University of New York Press, 1995), 59; Chaia Heller, 'For the Love of Nature: Ecology and the Cult of the

Romantic', in Greta Gaard (ed.), *Ecofeminism: Women, Animals, Nature* (Philadelphia: Temple University Press, 1993), 219–42.

18. Linda Vance, 'Ecofeminism and the Politics of Reality', in *Ecofeminism: Women, Animals, Nature*, 118–45; Chaia Heller, 'For the Love of Nature', 232.

19. Simone de Beauvoir, *The Second Sex*, trans H. M. Parshley (1949; London: Everyman, 1993), 406.

20. For an in-depth discussion of fluidity as metaphor, see Luce Irigaray, 'The "Mechanics" of Fluids', in Irigaray, *This Sex Which Is Not One*, 106–18.

21. Elizabeth L. Berg, 'The Third Woman', in *Diacritics*, 12:2 (1982), 17.

22. See Luce Irigaray, *I Love to You: Sketch of a Possible Felicity in History*, trans. Alison Martin (London: Routledge, 1996), 5.

23. See Margaret Whitford, *Luce Irigaray: Philosophy in the Feminine* (London: Routledge, 1991), 78.

CHAPTER 7. 'MIGHT BEFORE RIGHT': THE 1990s TRILOGY

1. See 'Edna O'Brien', an interview with Shusha Guppy, in George Plimpton (ed.) *Writers at Work: The Paris Review Interviews* (Harmondsworth: Penguin, 1986), 243–65.

2. See Nicholas Wroe, *Guardian*, 'Saturday Review', 2 October 1999, 6; Sophia Hillan King, 'On the Side of Life: Edna O'Brien's Trilogy of Contemporary Ireland', in *New Hibernia Review*, 4:2 (Summer 2000), 49–66.

3. It should in any case be acknowledged that O'Brien expressed concern about abortion law well in advance of the publication of *Down by the River*. In her 1990 interview with Julia Carlson, for example, she argues that 'No woman is overjoyed to have an abortion, but if she must have it, she should not be made to feel like a criminal'. O'Brien goes on to identify the refusal to women of 'access to information on abortion' as 'also a potential form of murder. Murder to the lives of women who are already born and trying to live their lives' (Julia Carlson, *Banned in Ireland: Censorship and the Irish Writer* (London: Routledge, 1990), 77). This can be linked to Irigaray's identification of cultural matricide.

4. Rebecca Abrams commented in her review of *House of Splendid Isolation* that: 'Josie clings stubbornly to the belief that beneath McGreevy's brutish appearance lies a heart of gold; all it needs is the love of a good woman to transform him into the handsome prince he really is. Instead of political, social or psychological

insight we are offered something that teeters dangerously close to *Beauty and the Beast*' ('Dangerous Places and Lunatic Times', *Guardian*, 17 May 1994). Abrams misses the point that 'romance' is a facet of patriarchal discourse, along with nationalism.

5. See Gerardine Meaney, 'Sex and Nation', in Ailbhe Smyth (ed.), *The Irish Women's Studies Reader* (Dublin: Attic Press, 1993), 233.

6. Significantly there is yet another echo of *Rebecca*, in which the eponymous character is assumed to be pregnant but is actually suffering from a malignant tumour. O'Brien, like Du Maurier, is concerned with social constructions of 'femininity' and 'maternity'.

7. See Andrea Dworkin, *Pornography: Men Possessing Women* (London: The Women's Press, 1981), 53.

8. Mary's response to the rape echoes that of 'Maya' in Maya Angelou's *I Know Why the Caged Bird Sings*. In the context of the woman writer's response to patriarchal culture, it is worth noting Christine St Peter's comment that many Irish women writers cite the influence of 'women writers from other traditions' such as Alice Walker and Toni Morrison (Christine St Peter, *Changing Irelands: Strategies in Contemporary Women's Fiction* (Basingstoke: Macmillan, 2000), 14).

9. See Robin Morgan, *The Demon Lover: On the Sexuality of Terrorism* (New York: Morton, 1989), 24.

10. See Margaret Ward, *In Their Own Voice: Women and Irish Nationalism* (Dublin: Attic Press, 1995), 46–7.

11. Meaney, 'Sex and Nation', 238.

12. In this context it is interesting to note that in 1916 Louise Gavan Duffy expressed her frustration at being 'sent up to the kitchen' to 'attend to the volunteers' instead of being allowed to fight (Ward, *In Their Own Voice*, 60).

13. In the context of the trilogy as a whole it is significant that Robin Morgan argues that because 'myth is simply another form of history, the encoded history of human beliefs' the links made by Yeats and Joyce between politics and myth help to reinforce the 'terrorist mystique' (Morgan, *The Demon Lover*, 53–5).

14. Clare Boylan, 'When Primitive Passions Remain Mired in the Past', in the *Express on Sunday*, 10 October 1999, 71.

15. Breege's rendering of the 'song that Bugler gave her' echoes Greta's response to 'The Lass of Aughrim', the song sung to her by Michael Fury, the lover who died for her.

16. Meaney, 'Sex and Nation', 230.

17. Significantly this is a syntactic echo of McGreevy's response to the birth of the calf – 'the impossible, licking love of it', reinforcing the contrast between animal and human maternities (*HSI* 15).

18. Meaney, 'Sex and Nation', 231.
19. Ibid.
20. Though the relationship is intertextually significant. The novel takes its title from Emily Brontë, and the doomed, landscape-dominated alliance of brother and sister does echo Cathy and Heathcliff in *Wuthering Heights*.
21. King, 'On the Side of Life', 65.
22. Nigel Edley and Margaret Wetherell, *Men in Perspective: Practice, Power and Identity* (London: Harvester Wheatsheaf, 1995), 157.
23. Mary Jacobus, *First Things: The Maternal Imaginary in Literature, Art and Psychoanalysis* (London: Routledge, 1995), 19.
24. Madeleine Leonard, 'Rape: Myths and Reality', in Ailbhe Smyth (ed.), *The Irish Women's Studies Reader* (Dublin: Attic Press, 1993), 107.
25. See Luce Irigaray, 'Women on the Market', in *This Sex Which Is Not One*, trans. Catherine Porter (Ithaca: Cornell University Press, 1985), 170–91.
26. Leonard, 'Rape', 107
27. Irigaray, *This Sex Which Is Not One*, 17.
28. King, 'On the Side of Life', 60.
29. Catherine Nash, 'Reclaiming Vision: Looking at Landscape and the Body', in *Gender, Place and Culture*, 3:4, 1996, 49.

CHAPTER 8. 'THE OTHER HALF OF IRELAND': *JAMES JOYCE*

1. See Shusha Guppy, 'Edna O'Brien', an interview in George Plimpton (ed.), *Writers at Work: The Paris Review Interviews* (Harmondsworth: Penguin, 1986), 249.
2. Anne Haverty, 'The Great Penman Who Burned to Be Betrayed', *Daily Telegraph*, 5 June 1999, 4.
3. John O'Mahoney, 'Iffy down the Liffey', *Guardian*, 26 June 1999, 10.
4. Guppy, 'Edna O'Brien', 256–7.
5. John O'Mahoney, 'Iffy down the Liffey'.
6. See Luce Irigaray, 'Equal or Different?', in *The Irigaray Reader*, ed. Margaret Whitford (Oxford: Blackwell, 1991), 30–33.
7. Irigaray's 'two lips' symbolism is analogous with the non-linear form of *écriture feminine* since she argues that the 'self-touching' which characterizes female genitalia 'give[s] woman a form which is in(de)finitely transformed without closing up on her appropriation'. This symbolism is also related to woman's access

to language and to communication between women; in 'When Our Lips Speak Together' – the title conflates genital and oral lips – Irigaray argues that: 'If we keep on speaking the same language together, we're going to reproduce the same history'. See 'Volume without Contours', in *The Irigaray Reader*, 53–67; 'When Our Lips Speak Together', in Luce Irigaray. *This Sex Which Is Not One*, trans. Catherine Porter (Ithaca: Cornell University Press, 1985), 205–18.

CHAPTER 9. *IN THE FOREST*: A COUNTRY BOY

1. Edna O'Brien, *In the Forest* (London: Weidenfeld and Nicolson, 2002).
2. David Godwin, letter to the *Irish Times*, 9 March 2002. Godwin is O'Brien's literary agent.
3. Fintan O'Toole, 'A Fiction Too Far', *Irish Times Weekend Review*, 2 March 2002, 1.
4. Ronan Bennett, 'The Country Girl's Home Truths', *Guardian Saturday Review*, 4 May 2002, 8.
5. In Greek myth Apollo punished Cassandra for rejecting his advances by endowing her with the ability to prophesy the truth, whilst simultaneously cursing her so that she would never be believed. Cassandra foretold the fall of Troy; she was ignored, and the city burned. Interestingly, the publisher's blurb to *In the Forest* likens the novel to Greek tragedy. In 1852 Florence Nightingale took the name 'Cassandra' for her polemic on the powerlessness of women in mid-Victorian society.
6. *Kinderschrek* translates literally as 'child shriek' or 'terror'; it is the German equivalent of 'bogeyman'.
7. Edna O'Brien, *Girls in their Married Bliss* (1964; Harmondsworth: Penguin, 1967, 119.
8. In keeping with the 'Cassandra' element of *In the Forest*, Eily's fate is prophesied even as the genesis of her rejection of materialism and enthusiasm for nature is revealed. She has met with a former lover at 'Kilcash ... the oldest of all the woods' (*IF* 43). The Edenic nature of this location is undermined by its name, incorporating 'kill' and 'Cash', the name given to Kate's son in *Girls in their Married Bliss* and an amalgam of 'Carlo' and 'Sasha', the names of O'Brien's own two sons. Maddie and his mother are killed directly by O'Kane, but indirectly by a society in which in Irigarayan terms the mother must be 'murdered' in order to ensure the survival of the phallic symbolic order.

9. Given the implications of Madge's role as nurturer and provider of 'space', O'Brien's presentation of this friendship is worth a chapter in itself; unfortunately the word limit on this study constrains further analysis.

10. See Mary Jacobus, *First Things: The Maternal Imaginary in Literature, Art and Psychoanalysis* (London: Routledge, 1995), 6–7.

11. I refer to statues such as that of Our Lady, said to have wept at the fall of Saigon in 1975. For a full account of such phenomena, see Marina Warner, *Alone of All Her Sex: The Myth and the Cult of the Virgin Mary* (London: Weidenfeld and Nicolson, 1976).

Select Bibliography

WORKS BY EDNA O'BRIEN

Novels

The Country Girls (London: Hutchinson, 1960; New York, Knopf, 1960; Harmondsworth: Penguin, 1963; London: Hutchinson Educational, 1971; London, Hutchinson & Co., 1972; London, Weidenfeld & Nicolson, 1981).

The Lonely Girl (New York: Random House, 1962; London, Jonathan Cape, 1962). Reprinted as *Girl with Green Eyes* (Harmondsworth: Penguin, 1964).

Girls in Their Married Bliss (London: Jonathan Cape, 1964; Harmondsworth: Penguin, 1967; New York, Simon & Schuster, 1968).

August is a Wicked Month (London: Jonathan Cape, 1965; New York: Simon & Schuster, 1965).

Casualties of Peace (London: Jonathan Cape, 1966; New York: Simon & Schuster, 1966; Harmondsworth: Penguin, 1968).

A Pagan Place (London: Weidenfeld & Nicolson, 1972; New York, Knopf, 1970; Port Townsend: Graywolf Press, 1984).

Night (London: Weidenfeld & Nicolson, 1972; New York: Knopf, 1973; Harmondsworth: Penguin, 1974; New York: Farrar, Strauss & Giroux, 1987).

Johnny I Hardly Knew You (New York: Doubleday, 1976). Reprinted as *I Hardly Knew You* (London: Weidenfeld & Nicolson, 1977).

Arabian Days (London: Quartet Books, 1977).

The Dazzle (London: Hodder & Stoughton, 1981).

The Country Girls: Trilogy and Epilogue (New York: Farrar, Strauss & Giroux, 1986).

The High Road (New York: Farrar, Strauss & Giroux, 1988; London: Weidenfeld & Nicolson, 1988; Harmondsworth: Penguin, 1989).

Time and Tide (New York: Farrar, Strauss & Giroux, 1992; London: Weidenfeld & Nicolson, 1992; Harmondsworth: Penguin, 1993).

House of Splendid Isolation (New York: Farrar, Strauss & Giroux, 1994; London: Weidenfeld & Nicolson, 1994; London: Phoenix, 1995).

Down by the River (London: Weidenfeld & Nicolson, 1996; New York: Farrar, Strauss & Giroux, 1996; London: Phoenix, 1997).

Wild Decembers (London: Weidenfeld & Nicolson, 1999; London: Phoenix, 2000).

In the Forest (London: Weidenfeld & Nicolson, 2002).

Collections of Short Stories

The Love Object (London: Cape, 1968; New York: Knopf, 1969; Harmondsworth: Penguin, 1970). Includes 'The Love Object', 'An Outing', 'The Rug', 'The Mouth of the Cave', 'How to Grow a Wisteria', Irish Revel', 'Cords' and 'Paradise'.

A Scandalous Woman and Other Stories (London: Weidenfeld & Nicolson, 1974; New York: Harcourt Brace Jovanovich, 1974). Includes 'A Scandalous Woman', 'Over', 'The Favourite', 'The Creature', 'Honeymoon', 'A Journey', 'Sisters', 'Love-child' and 'The House of My Dreams'.

Mrs Reinhardt and Other Stories (London: Weidenfeld & Nicolson, 1978; Harmondsworth: Penguin, 1980). Includes 'Number Ten', 'Baby Blue', 'The Small Town Lovers', 'Christmas Roses', 'Ways', 'A Woman by the Seaside', 'In the Hours of Darkness', 'A Rose in the Heart', 'Mary', 'Forgetting', 'Clara' and 'Mrs Reinhardt'.

Some Irish Loving (edited) (New York: Harper & Row, 1979; London: Weidenfeld & Nicolson, 1979; Harmondsworth: Penguin, 1981).

Returning: A Collection of Tales (London: Weidenfeld & Nicolson, 1982). Includes 'The Connor Girls', 'My Mother's Mother', 'Tough Men', 'The Doll', 'The Bachelor', 'Savages', 'Courtship', 'Ghosts' and 'Sister Imelda'.

A Fanatic Heart: Selected Stories (New York: Farrar, Strauss & Giroux, 1984; London: Weidenfeld & Nicolson, 1984). Collections of stories from other collections; previously uncollected stories included are 'Violets', 'The Call', 'The Plan' and 'The Return'.

Tales for the Telling: Irish Folk and Fairy Stories, illustrated by Michael Foreman (New York: Atheneum, 1986; Harmondsworth: Penguin, 1992).

Lantern Slides (London: Weidenfeld & Nicolson, 1990; New York: Farrar, Strauss & Giroux, 1990). Includes 'Oft in the Stilly Night', 'Brother', 'The Widow', 'Epitaph', 'What a Sky', 'Storm', 'Another Time', 'A Demon', 'Dramas', 'Long Distance', 'A Little Holiday' and 'Lantern Slides'.

Poetry

On the Bone (Warwick: Greville Press, 1989).

Published Plays

A Cheap Bunch of Nice Flowers, in *Plays of the Year*, ed. by J. C. Trewin (New York: Frederick Ungar, 1963).
A Pagan Place (London: Faber, 1973).
Virginia (London: Hogarth Press, 1981; New York: Harcourt Brace Jovanovich, 1981; San Diego: Harcourt Brace Jovanovich, 1985).
Zee and Co. (Harmondsworth: Penguin, 1971; London: Weidenfeld & Nicolson, 1971).

Screenplays

Girl with Green Eyes, adapted from *The Lonely Girl*, directed by Desmond Davies with executive producer Tony Richardson; a Woodfall production, released by Lopert Pictures, starring Rita Tushingham and Peter Finch, 1964.
Time Lost and Time Remembered, written with Desmond Davies from the short story 'A Woman at the Seaside'; directed by Desmond Davies and produced by Roy Millichip for Rank Organization, starring Sarah Miles, 1966.
Three Into Two Won't Go, adapted from the novel by Andrea Newman; directed by Peter Hall and produced by Julian Blaustein for Universal Pictures, starring Rod Steiger and Claire Bloom, 1968.
X, Y & Zee, from the screenplay *Zee & Co.*, produced at Shepperton Studios, London for Columbia, starring Elizabeth Taylor, Michael Caine and Susannah York, 1971.

Book-length Non-fiction

Mother Ireland, photography by Fergus Bourke (London: Weidenfeld & Nicolson, 1976; New York: Harcourt Brace Jovanovich, 1976).
James & Nora: A Portrait of Joyce's Marriage (London: Lord John Publisher, 1981).
Vanishing Ireland, photography by Richard Fitzgerald (London: Jonathan Cape, 1986).
James Joyce (London: Weidenfeld & Nicolson, 1999).

CRITICAL AND BIOGRAPHICAL STUDIES

Canadian Journal of Irish Studies: Special Edition on Edna O'Brien, 22:2 (December 1996).

Carlson, Julia, *Banned in Ireland: Censorship and the Irish Writer* (London: Routledge, 1990).

Carpenter, Lynette, 'Tragedies of Remembrance, Comedies of Endurance: The Novels of Edna O'Brien', in Hedwig Bock and Albert Wertheim (eds), *Essays on the Contemporary British Novel* (München: Max Hueber Verlag, 1986), 263–81.

Davies, Bonnie Lynn, 'Re-Constructing the Brick Wall of Phallocentric Discourse: Nell Finds Her M(Other) Tongue in Edna O'Brien's *Time and Tide*', in the *Canadian Journal of Irish Studies: Special Edition on Edna O'Brien*, 22:2 (1996), 73–82.

Duncan, Dawn, 'Edna O'Brien and Virginia', in the *Canadian Journal of Irish Studies: Special Edition on Edna O'Brien*, 22:2 (1996), 99–106.

Dunn, Nell, *Talking to Women* (London: Pan Books, 1996).

Eckley, Grace, *Edna O'Brien* (Cranbury, NJ: Associated University Presses, Inc., 1974).

Graham, Amanda, 'Comparisons: *The Color Purple* and *Down by the River*', in the *English Review*, 8:3 (February 1998), 20–23.

——'Edna O'Brien's "Mother Ireland"', in Glenda Norquay and Gerry Smyth (eds), *Space and Place: The Geographies of Literature* (Liverpool: Liverpool John Moores University Press, 1997), 97–110.

Graham, Amanda, ' "The Lovely Substance of the Mother": Food, Gender and Nation in the Work of Edna O'Brien', in *Irish Studies Review*, 15 (Summer 1996), 16–20.

Gramich, Katie, 'God, Word and Nation: Language and Religion in Works by VS Naipaul, Edna O'Brien and Emyr Humphries', in *Swansea Review* (1994), 229–42.

Grogan, Maureen, 'Using Memory and Adding Emotion: The (Re)Creation of Experience in the Short Fiction of Edna O'Brien', in the *Canadian Journal of Irish Studies: Special Edition on Edna O'Brien*, 22:2 (1996), 9–20.

Guppy, Shusha, 'Edna O'Brien', an interview in George Plimpton (ed.), *Writers at Work: The Paris Review Interviews* (Harmondsworth: Penguin, 1986).

Hargreaves, Tamsin, 'Women's Consciousness and Identity in Four Irish Women Novelists', in Michael Kenneally (ed.), *Cultural Context and Idioms in Contemporary Irish Literature* (Gerrard's Cross: Colin Smythe, 1988).

Haule, James, 'Tough Luck: The Unfortunate Birth of Edna O'Brien', in *Colby Literary Quarterly*, 23:4 (1987), 216–24.

Hillan King, Sophia, 'On the Side of Life: Edna O'Brien's Trilogy of Contemporary Ireland', in *New Hibernia Review*, 4:2 (Summer / Samhradh 2000), 49–66.

MacMahon, Sean, 'A Sex by Themselves: An Interim Report on the Novels of Edna O'Brien', in *Eire Ireland*, 2:1, 79–87.

O'Brien, Darcy, 'Edna O'Brien: A Kind of Irish Childhood', in Thomas Staley (ed.), *Twentieth-Century Women Novelists* (London: Macmillan, 1982), 179–90.

O'Brien, Peggy, 'The Silly and the Serious: An Assessment of Edna O'Brien', in *Massachusetts Review*, 28 (1987). 474–88.

O'Hara, Kiera, 'Love Objects: Love and Obsession in the Stories of Edna O'Brien', in *Studies in Short Fiction*, 30:3 (1983), 317–25.

Pearce, Sandra Manoogian, 'An Interview with Edna O'Brien', in the *Candian Journal of Irish Studies: Special Edition on Edna O'Brien*, 22:2 (1996), 5–8.

——'Redemption through Reconciliation: Edna O'Brien's Isolated Women', in the *Canadian Journal of Irish Studies: Special Edition on Edna O'Brien*, 22:2 (1996), 63–72.

Pelan, Rebecca, 'Edna O'Brien's "Stage-Irish" Persona: An "Act" of Resistance', in the *Canadian Journal of Irish Studies*, 19:1 (1993), 67–78.

——'Edna O'Brien's "World of Nora Barnacle"', in the *Canadian Journal of Irish Studies: Special Edition on Edna O'Brien*, 22:2 (1996), 49–62.

Quinn, John, *A Portrait of the Artist as a Young Girl* (London: Mandarin, 1990).

Rooks-Hughes, Lorna, 'The Family and the Female Body in the Novels of Edna O'Brien and Julia O'Faolain', in the *Canadian Journal of Irish Studies: Special Edition on Edna O'Brien*, 22:2 (1996), 83–98.

Salmon, Mary, 'Edna O'Brien', in Rudiger Imhof (ed.), *Contemporary Irish Novelists* (Tübingen, Gunter Narr Verlag, 1990), 143–58.

Schrank, Bernice and Danine Farquharson, 'Object of Love, Subject to Despair: Edna O'Brien's *The Love Object* and the Emotional Logic of Late Romanticism', in the *Canadian Journal of Irish Studies: Special Edition on Edna O'Brien*, 22:2 (1996), 21–36.

OTHER WORKS MENTIONED IN THE TEXT

Andermahr, Sonya, Terry Lovell and Carol Wolkowitz, *A Concise Glossary of Feminist Theory* (London: Arnold, 1997).

Beauvoir, Simone de, *The Second Sex*, trans. H. M. Parshley (London: Everyman, 1949, repr. 1993).

Berg, Elizabeth L., 'The Third Woman', in *Diacritics*, 12:2 (1982).

Boland, Eavan, *Object Lessons: The Life of the Woman and the Poet in Our Time* (London: Vintage, 1996).

Bristow, Joseph, *Sexuality* (London: Routledge, 1997).

Butler, Judith, *Bodies That Matter* (London: Routledge, 1993).

——'Performative Acts and Gender Constitution: An Essay in Phenomenology and Feminist Theory', in Katie Conroy, Nadia Medina and Sarah Stanbury (eds), *Writing on the Body: Female Embodiment and Feminist Theory* (New York: Columbia University Press, 1997).

Carter, Angela, *Shaking a Leg: Collected Journalism and Writing*, ed. Jenny Uglow (London: Vintage, 1998).

Cheney, Jim, 'Nature/Theory/Difference: Ecofeminism and the Reconstruction of Environmental Ethics', in Karen Warren (ed.), *Ecological Feminism* (London: Routledge, 1994), 158–78.

Cixous, Hélène, 'The Laugh of the Medusa', in Elaine Marks and Isabelle de Courtivron (eds), *New French Feminisms: An Anthology* (Brighton: Harvester Press, 1981), 245–64.

Coward, Rosalind, 'Female Desire: Women's Sexuality Today', in Mary Eagleton (ed.), *Feminist Literary Theory: A Reader* (Oxford: Blackwell, 1986), 145–8.

Deane, Seamus, *Strange Country: Modernity and Nationhood in Irish Writing since 1790* (Oxford: Oxford University Press, 1997).

Eagleton, Mary (ed.), *Feminist Literary Theory: A Reader* (Oxford: Blackwell, 1986).

Edley, Nigel, and Margaret Wetherell, *Men in Perspective: Practice, Power and Identity* (London: Harvester Wheatsheaf, 1995).

Friedan, Betty, *The Feminine Mystique* (1963; Harmondsworth: Penguin, 1965).

Gaard, Greta (ed.), *Ecofeminism: Women, Animals, Nature* (Philadelphia: Temple University Press, 1993).

Greer, Germaine, *The Female Eunuch* (1970; London: Granada, 1981).

Haberstroh, Patricia Boyle, *Women Creating Women: Contemporary Irish Women Poets* (New York: Syracuse University Press, 1996).

Hanson, Clare, ' "As a woman I have no country": Woolf and the Construction of national identity', in Tracey Hill and William Hughes (eds), *Contemporary Writing and National Identity* (Bath: Sulis Press, 1995).

——*Hysterical Fictions: The 'Woman's Novel' in the Twentieth Century* (Basingstoke: Macmillan, 2000).

Heron, Liz, *Truth, Dare or Promise: Girls Growing Up in the Fifties* (London: Virago, 1985).

Herr, Cheryl, 'The Erotics of Irishness', in *Critical Inquiry*, 17:1 (Autumn 1990), 1–34.

Hutcheon, Linda, *The Politics of Postmodernism* (London: Routledge, 1989).

Innes, C. L., *Woman and Nation in Irish Literature and Society, 1880–1935* (London: Harvester Wheatsheaf, 1993).

Irigaray, Luce, 'And the One Doesn't Stir Without the Other', in *Signs*, 7:1 (Autumn 1981), 60–67.

——*I Love to You: Sketch of a Possible Felicity in History*, trans. Alison Martin (London: Routledge, 1996).

——*Je, Tu, Nous: Toward a Culture of Difference*, trans. Alison Martin (London: Routledge, 1993).

——*This Sex Which Is Not One*, trans. Catherine Porter (Ithaca: Cornell University Press, 1985).

Jacobus, Mary, *First Things: The Maternal Imaginary in Literature, Art and Psychoanalysis* (London: Routledge, 1995).

Leonard, Madeleine, 'Rape: Myths and Reality', in Ailbhe Smyth (ed.), *Irish Women's Studies Reader* (Dublin: Attic Press, 1993), 107–21.

Light, Alison, ' "Returning to Manderley" – Romance Fiction, Female Sexuality and Class', in Mary Eagleton (ed.), *Feminist Literary Theory: A Reader*, 140–45.

Longley, Edna, *From Cathleen to Anorexia: The Breakdown of Irelands* (Dublin: Attic Press, 1990).

Macleod, Sheila, 'A Fairy Story', in Sara Maitland (ed.), *Very Heaven: Looking Back at the 1960s* (London: Virago, 1988).

Mantel, Hilary, *An Experiment in Love* (London: Viking, 1995).

Meaney, Gerardine, 'Sex and Nation: Women in Irish Culture and Politics', in *Irish Women's Studies Reader*, 230–44.

Modleski, Tania, *Loving with a Vengeance: Mass-Produced Fantasies for Women* (London: Methuen, 1982).

Moi, Toril, *Simone de Beauvoir: The Making of and Intellectual Woman* (Oxford: Blackwell, 1994).

Morgan, Robin, *The Demon Lover: On the Sexuality of Terrorism* (New York: Morton, 1989).

Murphy, Patrick D., *Literature, Nature and Other: Ecofeminist Critiques* (Albany: State University of New York Press, 1995).

Nash, Catherine, 'Reclaiming Vision: Looking at Landscape and the Body', in *Gender, Place and Culture*, 3:4 (1996), 149–69.

O'Connor, Mary, 'The Thieves of Language in Gaol?', in *Krino*, 15 (Spring 1994), 30–42.

O'Connor, Pat, *Friendships Between Women: A Critical Review* (Hemel Hempstead: Harvester Wheatsheaf, 1992).

Radway, Janice, *Reading the Romance: Patriarchy and Popular Literature* (London: Verso, 1987).

Rowbotham, Sheila, *A Century of Women* (London: Viking, 1997).

St Peter, Christine, *Changing Irelands: Strategies in Contemporary Women's Fiction* (Basingstoke: Macmillan, 2000).

Salleh, Ariel, *Ecofeminism as Politics: Nature, Marx and the Postmodern* (London: Zed Books, 1997).

Smyth, Ailbhe, 'The Floozie in the Jacuzzi: Intertextual Inserts', in *Irish Review*, 6 (1989), 7–24.

Smyth, Gerry, 'Being Difficult: The Irish Writer in Britain', in *Eire-Ireland*, Fall / Winter 1996, 41–57.

——'Irish Studies, Postcolonial Theory and the "New" Essentialism', *Irish Studies Review*, 7:2 (1999), 211–18.

Snitow, Ann Barr, 'Mass Market Romance: Pornography for Women is Different', in Mary Eagleton (ed.), *Feminist Literary Theory: A Reader* (Oxford: Blackwell, 1986), 134–40.

Ward, Margaret, *In Their Own Voice: Women and Irish Nationalism* (Dublin: Attic Press, 1995).

Warner, Marina, *Alone of All Her Sex: The Myth and the Cult of the Virgin Mary* (London: Weidenfeld and Nicolson, 1976).

Warren, Karen J., 'Towards an Ecofeminist Peace Politics', in *Ecological Feminism*, 179–200.

Whitford, Margaret, *Luce Irigaray: Philosophy in the Feminine* (London: Routledge, 1991).

Whitford, Margaret (ed.), *The Irigaray Reader* (Oxford: Blackwell, 1991).

Index

Recent and Forthcoming Titles in the New Series of

WRITERS AND THEIR WORK

RECENT & FORTHCOMING TITLES

Title	Author
Ivor Gurney	John Lucas
Hamlet 2/e	Ann Thompson & Neil Taylor
Thomas Hardy	Peter Widdowson
Tony Harrison	Joe Kelleher
William Hazlitt	J. B. Priestley; R. L. Brett (intro. by Michael Foot)
Seamus Heaney 2/e	Andrew Murphy
George Herbert	T.S. Eliot (intro. by Peter Porter)
Geoffrey Hill	Andrew Roberts
Gerard Manley Hopkins	Daniel Brown
Henrik Ibsen	Sally Ledger
Kazuo Ishiguro	Cynthia Wong
Henry James – The Later Writing	Barbara Hardy
James Joyce	Steven Connor
Julius Caesar	Mary Hamer
Franz Kafka	Michael Wood
John Keats	Kelvin Everest
Hanif Kureishi	Ruvani Ranasinha
Samuel Johnson	Liz Bellamy
William Langland: Piers Plowman	Claire Marshall
King Lear	Terence Hawkes
Philip Larkin	Laurence Lerner
D. H. Lawrence	Linda Ruth Williams
Doris Lessing	Elizabeth Maslen
C. S. Lewis	William Gray
Wyndham Lewis and Modernism	Andrzej Gasiorek
David Lodge	Bernard Bergonzi
Katherine Mansfield	Andrew Bennett
Christopher Marlowe	Thomas Healy
Andrew Marvell	Annabel Patterson
Ian McEwan	Kiernan Ryan
Measure for Measure	Kate Chedgzoy
Merchant of Venice	Warren Chernaik
A Midsummer Night's Dream	Helen Hackett
Alice Munro	Ailsa Cox
Vladimir Nabokov	Neil Cornwell
V. S. Naipaul	Suman Gupta
Edna O'Brien	Amanda Greenwood
Flann O'Brien	Joe Brooker
Ben Okri	Robert Fraser
George Orwell	Douglas Kerr
Walter Pater	Laurel Brake
Brian Patten	Linda Cookson
Caryl Phillips	Helen Thomas
Harold Pinter	Mark Batty
Sylvia Plath 2/e	Elisabeth Bronfen
Jean Rhys	Helen Carr
Richard II	Margaret Healy
Richard III	Edward Burns
Dorothy Richardson	Carol Watts
John Wilmot, Earl of Rochester	Germaine Greer
Romeo and Juliet	Sasha Roberts
Christina Rossetti	Kathryn Burlinson
Salman Rushdie	Damian Grant

RECENT & FORTHCOMING TITLES

Title	Author
Paul Scott	*Jacqueline Banerjee*
The Sensation Novel	*Lyn Pykett*
P. B. Shelley	*Paul Hamilton*
Sir Walter Scott	*Harriet Harvey Wood*
Christopher Smart	*Neil Curry*
Wole Soyinka	*Mpalive Msiska*
Muriel Spark	*Brian Cheyette*
Edmund Spenser	*Colin Burrow*
Gertrude Stein	*Nicola Shaughnessy*
Laurence Sterne	*Manfred Pfister*
Tennyson	*Seamus Perry*
W. M. Thackeray	*Richard Salmon*
D. M. Thomas	*Bran Nicol*
J. R. R. Tolkien	*Charles Moseley*
Leo Tolstoy	*John Bayley*
Charles Tomlinson	*Tim Clark*
Anthony Trollope	*Andrew Sanders*
Victorian Quest Romance	*Robert Fraser*
Edith Wharton	*Janet Beer*
Angus Wilson	*Peter Conradi*
Mary Wollstonecraft	*Jane Moore*
Women's Gothic 2/e	*Emma Clery*
Women Romantic Poets	*Anne Janowitz*
Women Writers of the 17th Century	*Ramona Wray*
Virginia Woolf 2/e	*Laura Marcus*
Working Class Fiction	*Ian Haywood*
W. B. Yeats	*Edward Larrissy*
Charlotte Yonge	*Alethea Hayter*

TITLES IN PREPARATION

Title	Author
Chinua Achebe	*Nahem Yousaf*
Ama Ata Aidoo	*Nana Wilson-Tagoe*
Matthew Arnold	*Kate Campbell*
Margaret Atwood	*Marion Wynne-Davies*
Jane Austen	*Robert Miles*
John Banville	*Peter Dempsey*
Pat Barker	*Sharon Monteith*
Julian Barnes	*Matthew Pateman*
Samuel Beckett	*Keir Elam*
William Blake	*Steven Vine*
Elizabeth Bowen	*Maud Ellmann*
Charlotte Brontë	*Patsy Stoneman*
Robert Browning	*John Woodford*
John Bunyan	*Tamsin Spargoe*
Cymbeline	*Peter Swaab*
Daniel Defoe	*Jim Rigney*
Anita Desai	*Elaine Ho*
Shashi Deshpande	*Amrita Bhalla*
Margaret Drabble	*Glenda Leeming*
John Dryden	*David Hopkins*
T. S. Eliot	*Colin MacCabe*
J. G. Farrell	*John McLeod*
John Fowles	*William Stephenson*
Brian Friel	*Geraldine Higgins*
Athol Fugard	*Dennis Walder*
Nadine Gordimer	*Lewis Nkosi*
Geoffrey Grigson	*R. M. Healey*
Neil Gunn	*J. B. Pick*
Geoffrey Hill	*Andrew Roberts*
Gerard Manley Hopkins	*Daniel Brown*
Ted Hughes	*Susan Bassnett*
Samuel Johnson	*Liz Bellamy*
Ben Jonson	*Anthony Johnson*
John Keats	*Kelvin Everest*
James Kelman	*Gustav Klaus*
Rudyard Kipling	*Jan Montefiore*
Charles and Mary Lamb	*Michael Baron*
Wyndham Lewis	*Andrzej Gasiorak*
Malcolm Lowry	*Hugh Stevens*
Macbeth	*Kate McCluskie*
Katherine Mansfield	*Andrew Bennett*
Una Marson & Louise Bennett	*Alison Donnell*
Merchant of Venice	*Warren Chernaik*
John Milton	*Jonathan Sawday*
Bharati Mukherjee	*Manju Sampat*
Alice Munro	*Ailsa Cox*
R. K. Narayan	*Shirley Chew*
New Women Novelists of the Late 19th Century	*Gail Cunningham*
Grace Nichols	*Sarah Lawson-Welsh*
Edna O'Brien	*Amanda Greenwood*
Ben Okri	*Robert Fraser*
Caryl Phillips	*Helen Thomas*

TITLES IN PREPARATION

Title	Author
Religious Poets of the 17th Century	*Helen Wilcox*
Revenge Tragedy	*Janet Clare*
Samuel Richardson	*David Deeming*
Nayantara Sahgal	*Ranjana Ash*
Sam Selvon	
Sir Walter Scott	*Harriet Harvey-Wood*
Mary Shelley	*Catherine Sharrock*
Charlotte Smith & Helen Williams	*Angela Keane*
Stevie Smith	*Martin Gray*
R. L. Stevenson	*David Robb*
Gertrude Stein	*Nicola Shaughnessy*
Bram Stoker	*Andrew Maunder*
Tom Stoppard	*Nicholas Cadden*
Jonathan Swift	*Ian Higgins*
Algernon Swinburne	*Catherine Maxwell*
The Tempest	*Gordon McMullan*
Tennyson	*Seamus Perry*
W. M. Thackeray	*Richard Salmon*
Three Avant-Garde Poets	*Peter Middleton*
Derek Walcott	*Stephen Regan*
Marina Warner	*Laurence Coupe*
Jeanette Winterson	*Margaret Reynolds*
Women Romantic Poets	*Anne Janowitz*
Women Writers of the 17th Century	*Ramona Wray*
Women Writers at the Fin de Siècle	*Angelique Richardson*